CORAL EMERSON

OPEN
THE DOOR
TO A
NEW YOU

4 KEYS to Unlock Your Life

Copyright © 2022 by **Coral Emerson**
Open the Door to a New You

Editor: Elaine Roughton
Cover design: Fiverr - germancreative
Photography: Milena di Latte Photography
Layout & formatting: Kingfisher Design

ISBN (Print): 978-0-6455045-0-7

All rights reserved. No part of this publication may be reproduced, distributed, or transmitted in any form or by any means, including photocopying, recording, or other electronic or mechanical methods, without the prior written permission of the publisher, except in the case of brief quotations embodied in reviews and certain other non-commercial uses permitted by copyright law.

Although the author and publisher have made every effort to ensure that the information in this book was correct at press time, the author and publisher do not assume and hereby disclaim any liability to any party for any loss, damage, or disruption caused by errors or omissions, whether such errors or omissions result from negligence, accident, or any other cause.

Adherence to all applicable laws and regulations, including international, federal, state, and local governing, professional licensing, business practices, advertising, and all other aspects of doing business in Australia or any other jurisdiction around the world is the sole responsibility of the reader and consumer.

Neither the author nor publisher assumes any responsibility or liability whatsoever on behalf of the consumer or reader of this material. Any perceived slight of any individual or organisation is purely unintentional.

The resources in this book are provided for informational purposes only and should not be used to replace the specialised training and professional judgement of a health care or mental health care professional.

Neither the author nor the publisher can be held responsible for the use of the information provided within this book. Please always consult a trained professional before making any decision regarding treatment of yourself or others.

The views expressed in this publication are those of the author alone and should not be taken as expert instruction or commands. The reader is responsible for his/her/their own actions, as well as his/her/their own interpretation of the material found in this publication.

DEDICATION

To my earth angels
The ones who challenge me
The ones who love me
This book exists because of you
Thank you for a dream come true

ACKNOWLEDGMENTS

I wish to thank my family for their constant belief in me and their love.

My mother for her wise words, my father for his kindness and my daughter for her enthusiasm and the light in her eyes that touches my soul.

For the wonderful people in this world who make it their life's work to help others, I honour you.

For my friends who said, "I need that!" when I spoke of my book.

For the one who taught me the hard lessons, broke my heart and became the inspiration to my own self transformation.

And for the gorgeous man who entered my life and showed me what true love was all about.

Thank you all for propelling my creative force!

WHAT OTHERS ARE SAYING

Coral has a beautiful way of showing you how much she cares about you and where you're at as you read through this book. I particularly loved the "Survival Checklist" that was offered right at the beginning of the book. This made me feel immediately at ease and that I already had a way to deal with things just a few pages in.

As I dived into the 4 Keys and the 4 Elements, I learned more about myself than I have in a long time. The combination of these keys and elements, in the steps they are laid out in, allows you to be gentle with yourself as you traverse the road to a whole new you while also showing you where you can push, just a little. I can't recommend this book enough!

– Lise Cartwright, Bestselling Author & Creative Business Coach

Some spend much or some of their life in a virtual room that at times can seem rather empty or sometimes even dark. Continually searching for that lamp in the corner or switch on the wall. Every now and then a slither of light gets through that little gap in the curtains to give them hope, but then as it does, it's gone again.

Satisfaction in life is a space we all hope for, but sometimes we're not sure how to achieve it. Everyone can do with a little help or a point in the right direction to find that door and leave that room to feel satisfied with their existence. Sometimes that's all they need. Someone saying to them "it's over here, there you are. It's now up to you"

Coral with her book 'Open the Door to a New You', could be that point in the direction you're searching for. After reading it I know there's something in there for everyone.

There's never a silver bullet, you always need to contribute to your own journey, but with the help of Coral and her experience in finding satisfaction and harmony in her own life, it's certainly worth taking notice of what this book has to offer.

It could be the light that will open the door to that room you feel you're in, to the rest of the house and then to the outside world.

It's an easy to understand read that could make that difference to your life.

– Ian Blackley, 6ix Radio Perth

It takes considerable courage to share traumatic lived experiences with others. It takes a lot of deep self-reflection to work through the lessons learned from these lived experiences. It takes a genuine love and concern for others around us to be willing to share these with the rest of the world.

In her book Coral displays this courage, deep self-reflection and genuine love for others. Having had a special 'other' in my life who was in some very dark places over many years, I have come to understand that in one's darkest moments we are not always brave enough or open to venturing on a journey of self-help. Coral's easy to read conversational writing style helps you to feel like there is a caring empathetic person sitting right there beside you having a chat and gently egging you on to make that first or next step towards creating a better place for yourself. Lots of simple tools, tips, checklists, and things to think about to help put you on your own self-help journey to becoming a better and more fulfilled version of you.

– Dr Robyn Morris (BA, Dip Ed, MA (Econs), PhD)

Having known Coral for more than three decades, I knew the depth of feeling this book would have before I read a word. If there is anything I would say about her, is that she has never changed in her depth of compassion for others and Open the Door to a New You *is a valuable case-in-point.*

This book offers simple signposts towards making life better in the more fast-paced lives we lead that seem somehow busier than ever and with increasingly less "me time". If that sounds like the change you need, then I suggest you have a good read. I can absolutely say Coral's messages come from a place of genuine care, mixed with the dose of reality she has lived in overcoming her own life adversities.

That means Open the Door to a New You *is nothing but real and maybe the best friend you will make this year*

– Steve Butler, Senior Reporter, The West Australian

CONTENTS

INTRODUCTION 1
SURVIVAL MODE 5
A DASH OF INSPIRATION 9
THE KEYS TO CHANGE 15
KEY 1: Realise 19
KEY 2: Release 63
KEY 3: Rebuild 87
KEY 4: Refine 113
CONCLUSION 131
DID YOU ENJOY THIS BOOK? 133
ABOUT THE AUTHOR 134
LINKS 135
NOW IT'S YOUR TURN 136

INTRODUCTION

Do you know that place where you simply exist and life feels like it has lost its magic?

Do you wish you had a way to move forward, to reclaim your life and make it sparkle and shine? Would you like to know how to go from simply *surviving* to *thriving*?

If yes, then I invite you to open the door to a new you and get access to the 4 Keys that will change your life forever.

From now on, within these pages you are with a friend. This book is going to pick you up from where you are and transport you to where you want to be.

I reach out my heart and my hand to you from a place of strength and love and courage, because I have been there too.

After experiencing one set-back after another, I found myself struggling to get back on track. At the point where I hit rock-bottom, I came to a realisation that I either had to stay there (no way!) or find the path out of the dark place I'd entered into.

Taking that journey changed my life and taught me more than I could ever have anticipated! It was tough, but so incredibly rewarding. If only I'd had a guide book to make things easier… but I didn't. I had a lot of other resources though and when I put them all together, I realised I had something special to share, something that could truly help others!

A massive transformation took place. It was so completely life-altering that I knew I couldn't keep it to myself. However, it was only when I started writing and seeing everything together in front of me that I realised there was a simple formula to the process.

I discovered that there were four main steps that I'd taken. These are the "4 Keys" that can be used in all of the crazy and challenging situations that life loves to throw at us.

You can use these Keys to help turn your life around and guide you to a place where you won't even recognise your old life any more.

Within these pages I share with you real life solutions and a balanced way to bring yourself back to being the *'you'* that you have always wanted to be!

You can do this... all it takes is a step in the right direction... I will show you how.

It is my sincere wish that after turning these pages you will turn over a new leaf in your life, never needing to look back, only forward with a happy heart.

It is possible to turn your life around in just a few months. That was my experience, and I was just working it out as I went along, without a guide book to help me. I totally believe in you. If you keep stepping forward you are going to experience something wonderful. Please don't wait any longer! You owe it to yourself to be best that you can be.

Do you want to live a happy, fulfilled, and fabulous life? Then start this journey now! What I will reveal to you will have long-term, life-changing results.

The best thing is, it's easier than you think! And you are stronger than you think... that is why you will succeed in creating the awesome life you've always wanted.

Take my hand, I am here with you every step of the way!

Love, Coral x

**Turn your life around
and open the door to a new you
with 4 simple Keys to success.**

SURVIVAL MODE

Before we go any further, I just want to check... how are you? If you're in a really bad place, stay with me.

Your well-being is the most important thing right now!

If you really are going through an awful time then this section is for you.

First of all: make sure you are in a safe place. You have the right to be safe, cared about, and respected. Take a look at your surroundings (and who you are surrounded by) and ask yourself if you feel safe. If not, grab this book and get the hell out of there!

You are about to embark on a journey where you are going to become the person you've always wanted to be. But you must be in surroundings that are positive (or at least neutral) to achieve this.

This is your first step to say, "Hey, I'm worth it! This is my life and I'm going to follow my heart and my dreams and live a happy, wholesome life, with nothing standing in my way!"

How does it feel saying that to yourself? Does it feel invigorating or a bit uncomfortable? That's okay. Whatever you're feeling is perfectly natural. If it's making you feel nervous, then you've just discovered the first thing standing in your way.

You.

Now, what would you tell your best friend if they were in a difficult situation? You'd encourage them to look after themselves. You'd want them to have an awesome, happy life, right? Well, from now on you need to be your own "best friend!" You deserve all the good things that everyone else deserves, and it is up to you to make that happen. I'll be here to help.

"Patience is a virtue." And that is so true. Often, we need to be a lot more patient... with ourselves in particular. Change takes time, but every small step towards it creates a giant leap closer to our goal.

We're only human, and sometimes we really get ourselves into a rut or fall into a deep dark hole. It happens to most of us at some point, and when it does, you do not want to stay there. Not a lot gets done when you're in that place, plus you feel awful and that's no good. I want you to feel great! And I'm sure you do too.

Think about this... you were born. That in itself is a miracle, a gift to the world. You are alive! Do you have any idea of how incredible you are? You are so unique, an amazing individual. It's time to celebrate everything that makes you who you are.

What we're aiming for here is the *best* of you, so that you can live your life to your full potential... where you can have enjoyment, pleasure, fulfilment, and the life you've always wanted. So stay with me, because this is where we're going on this journey together.

Your well-being comes first! Being safe and staying on the path towards health and happiness are essential... everything we will go through will flow naturally if you keep these important aspects in mind.

Doing anything proactive is better than being swallowed up by sadness. The trick here is either to break the cycle of *what you're doing* or what *your brain* is doing. So yes, when you need help, reach out for it. And don't stop reaching until you find it.

Okay, if things are pretty tough for you right now, let's look at some immediate options to help you get through it:

Survival Check List:

- Create your own safety net: have a list on-hand of services and people you can turn to
- Lifeline (or equivalent in your country), to call in time of need
- Doctor for advice and/or medication if required
- Counselling services
- Charitable services
- Relaxation techniques or meditation (audio is very helpful)
- Rescue Remedy, Bach Flower essences, pure essential oils (certified or homeopathic grade)
- Writing to release pent-up emotion (for your eyes only)
- Talking with someone you trust (create a list of people you know you can contact)
- Quiet time spent in solitude for peace, but also, just as importantly, social time spent with others… both are required for a healthy balance
- Relaxing shower, visualise washing your worries down the drain
- Play music that makes you feel good
- Bring pleasure back into your life by doing things you enjoy
- Spend time outside (or if weather prevents it, then somewhere different than normal)
- Keep busy!

Come back to this list any time you need to and add your own rescue remedies that work for you when times get tough.

I honour you and love your spirit. If you're thinking, "How can Coral say something like that? She doesn't even know me?" I don't need to... we are all brothers and sisters on this planet and it's about time we acted like it!

So, soul brother or sister, stay with me, because *who* you are right now can be transformed into the *you* that you want to be.

Let's go!

> *"Every journey starts with a single step."*
> —Lao Tzu

A DASH OF INSPIRATION

Is this book for you?

Well, if you want your life to be better, then YES!

We all have our own motivation to initiate positive change.

PAIN was my greatest MOTIVATION! Living with an injury from a car accident that happened a few years ago, I needed to find ways to live a full and happy life despite the pain. I not only wanted to get back to leading a relatively "normal" life, but I also went through a huge shift in my mindset where I realised I wanted to enhance my life to a far greater level than ever before. I knew there had to be something better... I just had to find a way to get there.

Well, I've done it! And I can tell you it was achieved through sheer determination and by taking very simple steps. I'm living with passion and loving life. I'm not going to let anything get in the way – especially myself.

If I can do it, you can too. We are all so different, of course; therefore we all have different ways of coping and reacting to the situations around us. Everyone has to heal in their own way. However, we *all* have the same choice to make change.

Now let me be straight down the line. I can't solve all your problems for you... no one can, except you. But I can give you the tools that worked for me. That is why

I've created this book: so that no matter what your personal situation is and whatever issues you need to deal with, you can pull information from here that will be relevant to you, and that you can adapt to your own situation. The one thing that remains the same, is that life is always better when we work on resolving those issues, rather than ignoring them. The power of choice is what we have in common… and the little choices in life can be the most significant and have the biggest effect on your well-being.

This book is like your best friend talking to you… I will be very honest with you, but always from a place of love!

Let me reassure you, how you choose to live your life is completely up to you. However, I am going to tell you what worked for me, and I'm going to be pretty very upfront about it, so take the parts that resonate for you and go with it.

Only a few months before I started to write this book, I was in such a state that I barely wanted to be alive… yeah, I was bad. However, I turned it around faster than I thought possible at the time. Now I not only have tremendous inner strength and determination, but also the systems in this book that I created to keep me on track if I ever go through a particularly challenging time again. The only way I was able to create it, was by *living* it, and clawing my way out of it. I can feel reassured that I will never find myself in that situation again. These are my life lessons, but if I can help even just one person, I am grateful.

It's time to set up your support systems – not only outside of yourself, but most importantly, within. To be at your strongest you need your own support system. *Something* you can turn to, rather than *someone*. Consider this: if *you're* always there for *you*, you'll never be alone in your struggles. Wouldn't it be great to know that you can trust in yourself to pull yourself through? Now, how empowering is that?!

Yes, that's the key to what may feel like a closed door. You are about to unlock your full potential by unlocking your inner strength. This is not about being selfish, but rather being self-aware. Be the kind of person you want to be. You don't think it's possible? Well, who's stopping you?!

Of one thing we can be sure: each of us is an individual. We need to respect – and accept – our individuality. Don't waste your energy trying to be like someone else or better than someone else. The jewel of this understanding is to be the best *you* can be! Now *that* is awesome!

Yes, circumstances change, things happen around us that are out of our control… but it's how we handle it that shows our true spirit.

When one door closes… and many others too - what do you do? From this book, I hope that you pick up what you want and place it into the shopping cart of your mind, so it's ready for you when you need it most.

I will share a little of my journey…

Then: I was struggling with pain from a car accident which happened a couple of years prior, carrying past issues which I hadn't addressed (but hadn't realised), unbalanced in heart, mind, body, and soul… I was highly stressed, my body was weak and exhausted, I had lost confidence in myself, and I fell into the abyss of deep sadness. I was in constant pain, almost broke, lost my job, my step-dad passed away, my relationship ended and I experienced the worst heartbreak I had ever known, and much more. This was all within just a few months. I'm afraid I was overwhelmed and I simply lost the joy in life. Within my soul I was in a deep dark place, broken, countless tears... but I can see now that I wouldn't have found what I was looking for if I didn't dig deeper. It was then that I found the treasure! And the treasure is me! Deep inside of you is your treasure too.

I had to break down. Which, in hindsight, I can see it meant I had to "break down" who I was... and start again. Now that takes the term "having a breakdown" to a new perspective!

Any challenging time is a time of transformation. Change is made possible when life becomes hard. Once you learn to grow from that experience you begin to understand the benefits of these challenges.

And now: happy, balanced, stable life, minimal stress, good pain management, confident and glowing, grateful for past challenges and where they have brought me to, following my dreams (sharing this book with you being a major one!), opening doors to great opportunities, thriving on new experiences, loving life!

What happened in between?

Well, what I share with you in this book is how I turned my life around.

In a nutshell, I made some drastic changes in my life so that I could overcome both the emotional distress, and the physical pain I was dealing with on a daily basis. If I couldn't deal with the pain, I simply wasn't going to have a good life. Now it doesn't mean the pain has gone, because it hasn't, but what it means is I approach it differently and I don't let it stand in the way of my own happiness and fulfillment in life.

I knew as I began my journey that first of all I would have to work out a way to get out of the deep dark hole I was in, as quickly and simply as possible. But in doing so I also wanted to find a way to create life-long change so that it would never happen again. That was really important to me.

To think that a few months prior to starting to write this book I had lost the joy in life because of how heavy my heart was, and then within months the transformation to where my heart was full, my life so vibrant and happy. How did this happen?

I *chose* it to happen! I set out on a path from which I would never turn back. Step by step, moving forward.

You do not need to make this journey on your own, but you alone must decide to make this journey.

Let's get you past where you are now and to where you need to be. I'm with you every step of the way.

This is not complicated, but yes, you do have to put some effort in. No reward comes from doing nothing.

I have narrowed this down to 4 KEYS

Yes, only FOUR! No complicated systems. Just a very easy check-list at the end of each chapter to help you keep on track. I didn't know the "keys" to turn my life around when I was going through all of this (wish I had!), but they became clear to me when I looked back… when I started writing this for you.

Let's begin

Are you loving life?! Are you feeling happy? If not – why not? It's time to ask yourself these raw and honest questions, as this will help shine a light on what it is you want to change.

Think about your life… are you feeling any of these things? Low, sad, depressed, anxious, worried, stressed, unsure, unhappy, unfulfilled, just ordinary, like it's all getting on top of you, or life is dull, boring, not how you want it to be. Or are you always fighting to get through life? Constantly coming across challenges and it just never seems to end? Right then, let's get started and turn this all around.

"Be an opener of doors."
—Ralph Waldo Emerson

THE KEYS TO CHANGE

**Open the Door to a New You with
Four Simple Keys to Success**

It's as easy as this:

FOUR KEYS

1. **Realise** – an awareness of where you are in your life and the changes you wish to make
2. **Release** – let go of what you don't need
3. **Rebuild** – build the life you want
4. **Refine** – enhance all that you have achieved

FOUR ELEMENTS

1. **Heart**
2. **Mind**
3. **Body**
4. **Soul**

The **4 Keys** of change require the acknowledgment of the **4 Elements** to be successful. This magical combination is what makes the 4 Keys to *lifelong* change successful.

The 4 Keys are made up of stages of awareness and actions that are designed to make this journey easy and achievable. Trust me, each step is vital. It sounds basic, but these really are the keys to positive change. Tackling each issue one step at a time, while honouring heart, mind, body and soul, is essential.

I'm going to cover some common topics here. These are the basics in getting your life, and yourself, in balance, and therefore they are a necessary component to moving forward in life. It's important that it's easy to read, but even more so, that it's easy to implement. Because that's the whole point.

The 4 Elements of **Heart**, **Mind**, **Body**, and **Soul** need to be within each Key. This is how you will achieve the balance you've been seeking. So to emphasise, the 4 Keys combined with the Elements of Heart, Mind, Body, and Soul, creates the magic combination that will get you to where you want to be!

For example, if I only focused on physio to treat the pain in my body (physical), I am not covering all aspects of the healing process. My heart, mind and soul (emotional, mental and spiritual parts of myself) have been affected by it too. So, to get the most out of the Keys, I need to remember to acknowledge all of the Elements.

As you begin your process, remember to consider your Heart, Mind, Body and Soul along the way, so that you can get a truly deep and meaningful experience with long-lasting results.

Start at the beginning and work your way through. I know, sounds simple, huh?! But it really is the best way to get the results you want, because each action in the process is there to make your progress to transformation successful. You may even like to take note of your achievements each step of the way, so you can look back and feel awesome.

You'll notice that each chapter gets smaller as you go

along. Why? Because the first step sets up for the next step, and so on. The main effort is required in the beginning, to get the ball rolling and the flow happening. After the first two stages it will get easier as you continue.

Like the base of a pyramid, set the foundations and lay the groundwork for the strength and resilience to come. As you travel through each stage there are simple, yet effective techniques to take you one step closer each time to where you want to be within yourself.

Whatever situation has got you to this place within yourself right now, take a good hard look at it. The obstacle that you dislike the most, that you don't want in your life, has been the catalyst for the most important change you're about to make.

If what you're doing isn't working, something will have to change. **You can do things exactly the same as you've always done and get the same result, or you can do something different and get a different result.** This book has been created from my own need to change my life… and now I share this knowledge with you to help guide you to your own inner resources to change your life forever.

So, grab a notebook and pen and get ready to turn your life around!

> *"What you decide, has the power to change your life."*
> —Coral Emerson

KEY 1

Realise

You must first realise things need to change, to proceed with change. The first step to resolving your issues is to realise what the issues actually are. Now is the time to become aware of what must change to create the life that you truly desire.

Ahead in this chapter are some very basic techniques to start turning your life around. Some nice, easy, and even fun ones!

This concept has two aspects to it… to both realise what those issues are *and* what to do about them. First, we'll look at realising your situation, so you know what you're dealing with. Then, step by step, how to approach common issues and work at regaining your strength.

So right now, it's time to look at your life, at what you are doing, what's around you, how you're feeling, and be real with yourself. Is this what you want for yourself?

Take a pause…

Think about where things are at in your life right now…

Ask yourself this question: "Is this working for me?"

If yes, great! It's a keeper.

If not, then you have these options:
1. **Fix it**
2. **Change it**
3. **Let it go**

From now on, any time that you're stuck on what you should do next, ask yourself that question and use that formula.

"Is this working for me?" If the answer is "No" or "Not sure", then choose to fix it, change it or let it go.

Examples:

"I've realised that my relationship is not healthy for me, but I don't know what to do." Fix it. Change it. Or let it go.

"My job is really stressful. I just don't think I can keep doing this." Fix it. Change it. Or let it go.

"I'm studying at university for the next 4 years, but I'm not sure this is what I want to do for the rest of my life." Fix it. Change it. Or let it go.

"My car keeps breaking down." Fix it. Change it. Or let it go.

As you can see, this formula works for so many different scenarios.

Listen to your intuition carefully and you will get the answer you need. This process is suitable for career choices, relationships, friendships, social activities, old habits and ways of thinking, and even on a materialistic level (very helpful when de-cluttering).

The simple difference between it getting fixed or not getting fixed is to ask ourselves: can we do anything about it? If so, great, more options are then available to us. What if it's something that can't be changed? Then we're better off accepting it and moving on. But *if* we *can* change it, and we *want* to? Then don't accept it – change it!

From now on it's important to recognise that when something concerns us, it means we have to do something about it if we want peace of mind. But what concerns you, me, your family, friends and everyone else, will be different for each individual. That's why this formula works.

If you're worried you don't have many options at the moment, then the *key* is to create options. How do you do that? Well, when you find that you've run out of choices, when all seems hopeless, what you have in fact are three options that *you* can create:

Funnily enough they are the same as the three above

Fix it – work at fixing the situation, find solutions to the problem, make improvements.

Change it – look at it from a different perspective, or find ways to alter the situation or outcome.

Let it go – Walk away from it. No more options needed for this situation any more, and it will open doors for other experiences and therefore new options.

So right now, you need to find what needs improving (within you and/or in your surroundings). And you need to be very honest with yourself. It's time to sort these dramas out. In fact, "drama" should be left on the stage and not brought into your life. One of my fabulous life lessons, haha!

Ask yourself, what is it that concerns you most? It's time to resolve your own issues. But to do that you need to recognise them.

Right, grab that pen and paper...

1. **Make a list of any issues currently in your life.**
Some common areas: health, relationships, family, finances, career, loneliness, anger, resentment, guilt, pain, depression, etc. Think of some that are bothering you right now and write them down.

2. **Next focus in on the specifics.**
Examples: Health - the main concern might be weight, or managing pain, or getting fitter. Career - it may be changing careers completely, or just changing one aspect, i.e., your role, going for a promotion, how to cope with work stress. Relationship - might be how to improve it, how to leave, or how to improve your relationship with yourself.

3. **Also write down what you want to improve in your life, and in yourself.**
Do you want more confidence? To be able to react more positively in negative situations? To deal better with pain? Heartbreak? Stress?

Note them all down...

You could do it in this format if you like: Grab a piece of paper and draw a line down the middle. On one side are the things you want to change, and on the other side are the things in your life that you love or make you feel good. Think of as many as possible for both. Keep pushing yourself and don't worry if any seem silly at first. Feel the freedom to express yourself and get it all out.

Now if you say something like, "I want to be happy," I encourage you to go deeper. What makes you happy? WRITE IT DOWN! Think of anything you like, it could be big or small - laying on the grass watching clouds, walking along the beach, visiting family, staying in a log cabin by a lake, a hot shower, eating chocolate, having the dream job (and describe what it looks like), a holiday overseas, BBQ with friends, the laughter of a child, a kiss from your partner, watching a really cool movie, a weekend away, writing a novel, Sunday drives, cuddles on the sofa, studying something you're passionate about, having a dog, an accomplishment at work, the sunshine on your face, stopping to smell the roses... ANYTHING AT ALL! What does happiness look like to you? It's going to be completely different for everyone, and only you really know what feels good for you. Have fun with this – use the senses – sight, sound, smell, touch, taste – and use your imagination! Don't hold anything back. This is just for you and you alone.

Step 1: Write as many down as you can think of, positives and negatives (remember to leave a little bit of room to add extra ones in later when you think of more). Go for it!

Step 2: How do you go about achieving these things? If it all seems a bit overwhelming, then just choose one! Pick one of the most important items on your list, something you would like to happen soon, or at least be working towards as soon as you can. So that's it, just pick one.

And be sure to use the processes in this book to knock through them one by one. Don't let any obstacle stand in your way of the life you want. Because the greatest obstacle of all... is ourselves!

Now is also the time to question your standards and values. Do they enhance your life or hold you back?

Realisation is the key to all that is to follow. You need to be true to yourself.

Now let's get everything sorted, step by step.

You may be wondering, is this experience going to be easy or hard? Well, for the most part, the solutions are quite simple, but along the journey there will be some challenges. **Without challenges, there is no change.** The challenges you face, and the ones you come across as you travel with me now, will ultimately bring reward. Right now, taking the step forward to change is the most important thing in your life. You are the most important thing in your life!

Change happens whether we want it to or not. So, let's direct it where we want it to go.

Listen to your intuition. When you're pushing yourself in an unnatural direction, things feel wrong.

Some good questions to ask yourself when you're feeling unsure:

- Is it wrong, or right?
- Heavy or light?
- Good or bad?

Or ask yourself: "Do I want to feel better, or do I want to feel worse?"

"Well, I want to feel better, of course!" This can help to clarify the decision-making process.

There will be a feeling, a gut instinct, an intuition... sometimes it will be really obvious, and at other times it may only be a subtle sensation. *Trust in this, trust in yourself, for it is only you who knows what is right for you.*

Others will have opinions, but remember, that is their opinion, their judgment from their position. Not yours. Your greatest strength will be in making your own decisions. And making ones that work in the direction of where you want to go.

Ask yourself, "Does this decision contribute positively to the path I want to be on?" If yes, yippee! If not, look at other options until it does.

So, first of all, start with the recommendations in the next few pages. You don't need to do *everything* all at once. Let's start with these basic few steps and everything else will flow on from there.

> "Treasure yourself. Treasure your body. It's what holds you together, after all."
> —Coral Emerson

Firstly, let's deal with your health.

If your health is causing you trouble, it is going to be a heck of a lot harder to fix everything else. You need to make this your priority right now!

So, it's time to deal with those health issues. Your health plays an important part in how you feel, how you function, how you deal with everything else in your life, and your overall quality of life. For some people, their health issues are merely a slight nuisance, for others it plagues them every day and can be quite detrimental. Sometimes we live with it so much or for such a long time that we "get used to it." Well, that's just not good enough! Trust me, I've been there, and the best thing I could've done was to make my health a priority and to keep seeking advice and assistance if and when I require it.

Doctor:

Make a list of all the health issues you would like to fix. Take that list with you to your doctor – tell them you are serious about a lifestyle change; that your health is important to you, and you seek their advice and support. Be determined and your doctor will sit up and notice. Perhaps you may like to take a supportive friend or partner with you to help give extra strength behind what you want to express.

Often those closest to us are affected by this too... and if we treasure our loved ones, then that is another good reason to start treating our bodies with the love and care they deserve. It's important you have a doctor that you respect and trust and can discuss anything with. If you don't have one yet, please take the time to find one. Ask friends and people in your region for their recommendations on local doctors and that will give you a good idea of who you might like to visit.

Whatever you need to improve upon in your health, do not stop and do not give up. You are worth it. Sometimes, we exhaust all avenues of being able to fix the problem entirely; for example, serious illness, chronic conditions or long-term pain. When this is the situation, then a different approach is sometimes needed. If you know there is nothing more that can be done (at this present time with the most up-to-date medical knowledge), then it is very important to find a way to shift your focus. In fact, this is vital.

Now, once you've taken that first step, and your doc is helping you as best they can, it is still up to you to progress forward with your health. Don't stop there. If need be, seek out other health professionals and alternative therapies that suit *you*, and what your body needs the most.

Remember to keep up with regular appointments, such as the dentist and skin cancer specialist. Prevention is better than cure! The investment in yourself, and particularly your health, will be the greatest investment you've ever made. After all, this body is the only vessel to house our soul at the moment, and it's our honour and responsibility to look after it

And for anyone battling with drugs, I have one thing to say: Turning to drugs is like turning to your enemy for support. Seek help immediately. If you want to go on this journey you need to be drug-free.

Take care of your health and everything else will flow much more easily.

Sleep:
The quality of your sleep is essential to your progress. It's time to respect your body's need for rest, for the chance to recuperate. If sleep is an issue in any way, make it a priority to fix it immediately! I cannot emphasise this enough.

There are many resources out there: books, magazines, sleep professionals and literally a world-wide web of information. Find what works for you. There are lots of natural methods that can assist you: relaxation techniques, meditation, herbal teas, essential oils, understanding your sleep pattern, setting your alarm to create a routine, avoiding trigger foods that keep you awake, time out from digital devices (ie computer or smart phone) in the lead-up to bedtime, pen and paper beside your bed to let go of repetitive thoughts during the night, exercise during the day, and so much more.

Don't ignore this step. If you want to live a happier and more vital life, this truly is a very important aspect to it. It's an essential part of your healing and strengthening process. Establish a good sleep pattern. If you can get that under control, then everything else will be so much easier. It *is* possible to re-set your internal body clock if it has gone off track. There is a lot of information about this out there, and professionals who can help also, so if this is troubling you, then don't hesitate a moment longer and get it fixed!

Good sleep is a priority. Without it the following can occur:

- Depleted immune system (negatively affects the immune system)
- Weight gain (hunger and cravings have been known to be affected by poor sleep)
- Increased stress levels
- Lack of concentration
- Deprived cognitive function
- Aching muscles
- Excessive fatigue
- Decreased motivation
- And much more...

Make your bedroom a haven, somewhere that you look forward to going for rest, relaxation, and a good night's sleep! A comfortable, clean, and relaxed space. Dim and quiet, with no (or at least minimal) technology in room. Start making preparations for sleep half an hour before you intend to go to bed, giving yourself time to get ready and also time to settle.

And whenever things go off track for you, come back to making sleep your priority.

"Today is about living the day, and moving forward in life"
—Coral Emerson

Good morning:
"The way I start my day sets its tone. When I make the decision to begin by giving thanks for the positive things in my life, no matter how seemingly few or bountiful they might be, I am setting the flow for new opportunities to come my way."
—Josh Hinds, Author and Speaker

So true. Having a morning routine that gets you off on the right path for the day is always helpful. It sets the tone for how you're going to deal with the day.

Every morning I give thanks for the day ahead, and put positive thoughts out there towards what I want to achieve for the day. I also take a moment to think of others, to wish them good health and happiness, especially anyone I know who is going through a hard time. I prepare myself to accept what the day brings and remind myself that I can cope with anything that comes my way, because who knows what may happen on that day? This is done within just a few minutes, and is incredibly grounding.

Get up and explore this day! The mystery of life is still something we should all be blessed to wake up to!

If your morning routine is chaotic, look at ways to make it flow better so that it contributes to a more satisfying day.

"Look for the sunshine in each day. It is there to be found. It is within you. Tap into its warmth and light, and breathe energy into your soul."
—Coral Emerson

Activity:

Otherwise known as exercise!!! But let's not go overboard here.

Right now you need to get active – but start at a pace you're comfortable at, and start with activities you enjoy! As my mother says: "Get out and go for a walk." Seems so simple... and yet, it's actually one of the best bits of advice ever. The difference between crying in your pillow and sitting around feeling down, to getting out into the fresh air, is *huge*! A walk takes you out of the situation you're in. It also gives all of your senses something else to notice. It's an easy and natural way to start building on your fitness, health, and confidence. If you're stuck indoors due to the weather then a simple change of scenery can also be very helpful.

Choose any activity that is enjoyable to you right now, start doing it! Get your body moving and an energy flow back into your heart and soul.

When it comes to fitness, choose a level that is suitable for you, nobody else. You're not trying to be like anybody else, but instead adapt to where your body works the best for you, so that your body gives you more value. There are so many variants when it comes to fitness, but the important thing is, what do *you* want to get out of it? What are the benefits to you?

For some it is weight loss or health, for others to look toned, and for most it is to *feel* good.

If you are already naturally active, sporty, or fit, then keep it up. But make sure you include activities that you enjoy. Physical activity creates a positive mindset – particularly if you're having a great time!

It is also scientifically proven to increase endorphins (happy feelings). How good is that?! If it's simply just getting outside and doing something you enjoy, it's a win-win situation all round.

Suffering from pain from a car accident, I understand that we can't always rush these things. If you have physical pain, a medical condition, illness, damage, or any other restrictions, after the initial discussions with your doctor, seek the advice of a physiotherapist (or similar), and they will assist you with a guided program made especially for you. Taking this one step further in improving your health will make a tremendous change in your life. But you must be willing to follow the program. You are worth it. Yes, I'm writing to YOU right now! YOU ARE WORTH IT!!!

> *"Out of the darkness and into the sunlight."*
> —Coral Emerson

And while you're at it, you can soak up the benefits of sunlight, getting a good dose of Vitamin D. As an Aussie, the "sun smart" message is ingrained in me, so just a precaution to please use sun protection. But yes, a little ray of sunshine goes a long way. Being outside surrounded by plants and nature greatly increases the feel-good triggers too. There is everything to be gained from getting out and about and your body moving.

Write down some activities that you like doing:

- ....
- ....
- ....

> *"Let food be thy medicine."*
> —Hippocrates

Food:

Our relationship with food is a mirror to our relationship with life. Are you feeding your body the fuel it needs?

Are there beautiful essential nutrients flowing through you... or gunk?! Well... this is a biggie!! You need to enjoy what you eat. But your body needs to enjoy it too. If you want to be at your best, then *give* yourself the best.

This aspect of my own journey has been life-changing! I am astounded at how my health has improved from making a few simple adjustments to my diet. I have more energy and vitality, my skin has improved, and overall, I look and feel better than ever before. All because of respecting my body and making a healthy choice of food and drink that nourishes me rather than draining me. Well worth it, I can tell you!

It is definitely worth your time to look more deeply into what foods are actually good for you and what leaves you feeling sluggish. Diets high in processed foods cause many issues, and can create terrible inflammation in our system. Inflammation contributes to an increase in pain and physical discomfort, as well as a lot of problems most of us wouldn't have even realised, including anxiety, feeling unhappy, and generally unwell. Also, we are often unaware that we are simply lacking essential vitamins and minerals. If you want to be vibrant, healthy, and the best you can be, then it is vital go on this journey to rediscover the joys of food and its true purpose in our lives, the incredible healing powers that nature has provided, and the benefit of a body that gives you back the best.

Please do not deny this part of the process, for it is absolutely essential for the healthy and happy future you are aiming for.

There is a lot of information out there to guide you with making the right food choices, and a good nutritionist can provide personalised support.

This is my favourite smoothie recipe. I find that it helps to keep my energy levels consistent throughout the day.

GREEN SMOOTHIE

1 banana
1 cup frozen mango
¾ cup baby spinach
2 tsp plant protein powder
1 tsp maca powder
¼ tsp turmeric blend
¼ tsp acai powder
¼ tsp spirulina
¼ tsp natural vanilla extract
1 cup almond coconut milk unsweetened

Blend and serve

Notes: You can adapt this recipe to suit your taste. Other fruit that I sometimes add in are pineapples and/or strawberries. Just bear in mind though, as soon as you add berries, it won't be very "Instagrammable"! Pink or purple tones blended with green, yeah it's not pretty – but it tastes great!

The turmeric blend is: cinnamon, turmeric, nutmeg, ginger, pepper.

My favourite turmeric blend is *Turmeric Latte* from Turmeric Direct and my preferred protein powder is *Earth Protein* Natural Rice and Pea Protein Vanilla from Bulk Nutrients. I've put the links at the back of the book.

"What you think, you become."
—Buddha

Mindset:

I bumped into a friend recently and asked, "How was your holiday?" Her face suddenly dropped, "Back to reality," she said. I paused, and replied, "Then your reality needs changing!"

Almost everything that's going on within us links back to our mindset. And it's our mindset that needs to change if we are to create positive change.

Okay, to start with, this is a quick aide to help you get out of a tough spot. Let's swap negatives with positives. Negative thought? Immediately swap it with a positive thought. Make it a game with yourself: the funnier or sillier, the better – it just has to break the first thought and replace it! Yes, it's only temporary, but it does have good results, and the more you do it the more natural it becomes. Later on, you will have more tools to go above and beyond this.

While I was going through a difficult time and fighting my old reactions to things that got to me, I also came up with these two sayings:

"Science Experiment"

For example, imagine if you lived with house-mates who are extremely dirty and messy and you're clean and tidy. Obviously, this is very frustrating and if communicating with your house-mates doesn't result in any improvement then it's necessary to find another way around it.

Now I've been in this situation and my first reaction was that I wanted to clean absolutely everything so I could have peace of mind. But running around after other people and cleaning up their mess is not the appropriate action to take when strengthening who you are as a person. So... instead, despite my natural desire to want to fix it, I learned to take a step back from the scene, look at that mountain of their dirty dishes and the unknown green object growing in the corner, and find amusement in the fact that it's a: "Science Experiment!"

I admit it, I've done it and it worked! Oh, it was not easy I can tell you. My desire to step in and do it myself was very strong. But I had my own lessons to learn here. I had to remind myself that I wasn't put on this Earth to be cleaning up after them and I needed to re-set my natural behaviour in that particular circumstance. Adding humour to something unpleasant, as well as removing yourself from the situation, helps to break its effect on you. Besides it's not your mess to worry about, you just have to, um, step around it, so to speak.

"A Learning Journey"

When you just can't work out what the heck is going on or *why*! Remind yourself this is simply part of your spiritual journey or a learning journey… and everything becomes easier instantly. So, when things get a little crazy, think to yourself, "It's all part of my learning journey." Basically, something difficult sent to help you grow. Remember that growth brings with it a certain level of discomfort, but also great reward.

Another example of a common situation is someone saying something to you that is negative and it makes you want to react, and perhaps even come back with fighting words… instead, take a breath and think "What is the lesson I'm learning here?" It might simply be to remain calm in challenging situations, and if so, that's a great lesson.

Now these suggestions are for when you need to remove negative emotion or reactions *quickly*. However, for long-term benefits you will gain greater success once you have gone through all of the stages in this book. But keep these two sayings handy and use them whenever you need: *Science Experiment* and *Learning Journey*.

Negative self-talk is the one thing that can destroy you if you let it. So don't let it. Use all of the resources you have to combat this and it will get easier the more you practice it.

> *"Look to the horizon. There you will see more than you ever saw before."*
> —Coral Emerson

Here's another tip. It's a physical one, but it has an empowering impact on your brain.

When you go outside, or go for a walk, most of us just look at what's around us, perhaps a little bit further, but quite often it's literally what's immediately in front of us (so we don't trip as we're walking!). This is a great one to try:

"Expand Your Horizons"

Look at the horizon, or as far as you can see. As you go along, keep bringing your attention back to stretching your vision as far as it can go. In doing this you are also stretching your mind, you are opening up your own horizons, taking the internal out into the external. You are allowing yourself to look beyond, to go outside of your normal thought processes and your "vision" of what you think your life should be. It's a very simple but powerful tool, and is particularly helpful in getting out of a restricted mindset, besides being a pleasure to appreciate the view around us with more mindfulness.

If you're stuck indoors due to weather or work commitments you can still use this trick, looking out the window as far as you can, or across the room. Focus on things that you don't normally notice and stretch your vision to see things differently. I hope you find it helps.

On emotions, I will share something with you, because this has been a difficult part of the journey for me, as it is for anyone going through a hard time.

I will admit to you I'm a sensitive person, and it's a bittersweet attribute. I *feel* things so strongly! Not just my own feelings, but those of others around me too. Perhaps you do as well, or know someone else who does. Trust me, it can be very draining. But on the upside, it allows for great empathy, thoughtfulness, kindness, and understanding.

It has taken a lot of effort to respect and understand my sensitive side while also strengthening my resilience. It can be a really awkward journey if you don't accept and appreciate who you really are. But I found the methods that worked for me and I have achieved that. This doesn't mean I don't feel emotions like I used to. I still feel them! What it means is that I won't let my emotions rule me, or ruin me. The effort taken to change my former mindset has been well worth it. In fact, it's been life-changing.

Believe me, putting a big portion of your time and energy into this is going to be well worth it for you too. Any positive change to your mindset not only helps to diminish stress, but it will also open doors to positive growth. And positive growth brings a happier and more fulfilled life.

There are a lot of books on this subject, which are very helpful. For me, I found knowledge from books, combined with visiting a clinical psychologist (referred following the car accident), and having a couple of sessions of professional hypnotherapy, to be a fantastic trio that resulted in a tremendous turnaround in mindset.

> "People feel GUILTY for questioning their career, marriage, dedication, "status" in life, and feelings. It's also UNCOMFORTABLE. But that examination is the first gate to self-awareness and then - if you drop the guilt and add an action plan - growth!"
> —Brendon Burchard

Talking:

It's good to get it out...

When times are tough and everything just keeps going around and around in your head, it can be really helpful to be able to talk it out with someone else. This is not a journey that you have to struggle with by yourself, and sometimes it just all gets to be too much. Choose a person you trust and feel free to express your concerns and worries with, as this will help to lift the weight from your shoulders. Simply having a kind listening ear can be very soothing to the soul. Plus, gaining another perspective can also be extremely helpful.

If possible, I would highly recommend a professional in this field, for example a counsellor or a clinical psychologist. This is a wonderful option if you've got some tricky issues to tackle as they have years of experience and some clever tools to assist you.

A life coach or mentor is another option. This approach can be somewhat different; a life coach or mentor will tend to focus more on the here and now, and the future, helping you to push through the barriers that are holding you back. Depending on your personality, or your goals, this could be a fantastic option to consider.

Here in Australia, we have a good healthcare system. Although you often have to ask for help outright to get the ball rolling. The best way to do this is to get a mental health care plan and a referral to a clinical psychologist from your doctor as soon as you can and get right onto it. I resisted this idea at first as I thought it was a bit drastic; I had constant pain in my back and trouble coping with it. Was that really the path I needed to go on? Well, as it turns out, yes. As specialists in their field, they really know how to unlock the real issues and to knock your problems out of the water and get real results!

If you don't want to go that deep, but feel you would benefit from talking to someone, perhaps seek a qualified counsellor. Be reassured that all qualified counsellors and clinical psychologists are confidential and non-biased, and you are free to express everything that you need to.

Unfortunately, not all countries have the same level of healthcare, and for some the option of turning to a professional may be out of reach. Please don't let that stop you… there will be someone with a kind heart who will be happy to listen.

If you truly get stuck finding someone to talk to, then writing it all down can help too. Get it out. Privately though, this level of expression is not to share on social media. Remember, the written word, once put out there, is out there forever. Instead, you simply want to get it out, release it, let it go or find ways to resolve it, and move on.

> *"If you have made mistakes, even serious mistakes, you may have a fresh start any moment you choose, for this thing we call "failure" is not the falling down, but the staying down."*
> —Mary Pickford

Cry:

Hey, if you need to, you need to. And that's that. This time will pass. Don't shake your head, "No, it won't." IT WILL! Tears are allowed to flow. It is a natural release of held-in emotion. On a physiological level, cortisol (stress hormone) is released via the tears, therefore crying can also help relieve stress.

Be reassured that this is for now, not forever.

> *"Home is where the heart is."*
> —Gaius Plinius Secundus

Home:

Are you living somewhere that you love?

Do you feel safe and secure, comfortable? Is it a positive environment for you, right now and in your future? Does it aid in your growth towards the person you want to be?

If you answered yes, then all good.

If no, then it could be time to consider a change: either the situation you're in or the area in which you live. You need to be able to look at this with new eyes and be very honest with yourself. If it's no good for you, walk away from it and start afresh. You deserve more! You deserve to live somewhere that is positive and wholesome for your heart, mind, body, and soul. It is essential to have a sanctuary to go to... and that is your home.

> *"Your vibe attracts your tribe."*
> — Chris Ducker

Family and Friends:

Your loved ones are the most precious resource and greatest support.

Write a list of people who you can rely on at any time. This might only be one person, or just a few... it's not the amount that matters. It is the quality of the person at the other end – right when you need them.

Family and friends understand you the most. Let them enfold you with their loving arms and warm support when you need it. You would do the same for them, right? And you would feel so glad that you could help someone else. Well, they feel like that about you too.

If you are a parent, I know you're going to be incredibly busy, and you might think, "…but I don't have time for this!" However, consider what your actions and life choices are telling your children. To have them seeing you making positive changes in your life, making your well-being a priority, choosing to be happy and living life to the fullest, is going to be incredibly inspirational to them too! The best way for children to learn is to observe. Actions really do speak louder than words. When you set an example of working your way out of a challenging situation and turning it into a better one, then you're showing them not only what you can achieve, but what they can achieve too. This will resonate with them for the rest of their life.

On this part of your journey, what you are doing at the moment is finding out what works for you and what works against you. Your friends and family are there for you, but there are times when they may feel unsure how to help you best. Plus, they don't know *everything*!

And you can't expect them to. They are there to be your support, but you must be your own strength.

When it comes to specific problems, often the best thing you can do is to turn to someone who is trained in that specific field. They are the professional; therefore they can assist you best with that particular issue. You wouldn't turn to a mechanic for advice about your teeth, or a Sumo wrestler for tips on how to get a toned butt! Someone who is already trained in a specific field and is experienced in this line of work is naturally the best source for any information and assistance. Friends and family can offer advice for sure, and often it is highly valuable. But remember, they are not experts on all of your issues (neither should they have to be). Share with them by all means, but take it on board yourself to resolve your own issues. You will feel tremendously empowered by this one decision!

Sometimes family and friends feel more comfortable with you the way you are, but remember that although they may have loving intentions, it's your life! Some decisions we make are not what people expect we'll make... and that's okay. In fact, it's not only okay, it's brilliant, because it's *your* decision and it is important *to you*. You will feel so uplifted in yourself for doing this. Now consider if you want to make a big decision... and you don't want anyone to talk you out of it... well, don't tell anyone! Just do it!

When I decided I wanted to write a book, it was somewhat nerve-wracking, but also very empowering. When you know that you can cope with things on your own – do them on your own. It will be very rewarding. When you can't cope – ask for help. Don't give up until you have the help you need (whether it's from your own inner strength or the assistance of others).

Alternatively, if you find yourself in a position where it

is you who is being relied upon by family and friends, and it is draining you, remember this: it is not your job to unburden someone of the decision they make (no matter how close they are to you, how nice a person they are, and how much you love them). Don't take on the guilt – it is not yours. Instead, be the best support you can be. Stand by their side and love them, absolutely yes, but allow them to take responsibility for themselves. Their burden is not yours to carry.

If you have trouble with this, seek advice or information on how to strengthen your resolve and change the balance, and most importantly for your own sake, your mindset, so that you are no longer affected by this. Know that it is possible to honour your own needs while also caring for those around you. In strengthening your own self-worth, you will have even more energy to give and share, helping those you care for the most. The greatest love is in respecting others' choices, and in respecting your own.

Regrets – they're a waste of time and energy. If you have trouble with this, please seek help with it, otherwise it's going to eat you up until you come to terms with it. Move on – let it go. Repeat. A very common saying "in hindsight", is used frequently in our society; however, consider this... the only reason we have "hindsight" is because we've gone through the experience in the first place. So when hesitating, making a decision is better than to make no decision at all. Even if you *decide* not to make a decision, haha, that's great! And when you do make that decision, remember it can always be changed along the way if need be, but at least a direction has been taken, and that is a very powerful force for other things to flow your way. And if it is the right direction, it will flow beautifully!

I saw this and just had to share with you, as it has significant relevance to the subject of friends and family for some people. I met Michael, *The Mojo Master*, and he has quite a dynamic personality. He provides a very interesting insight below:

> *Who you hang around is who you become.*
> *This is a well-known success principle for many who are living the life they designed.*
> *It is hard to break away from many friends who may hold you back. It's not easy as you may be judged or outcast from the friendship groups and circles that brought you many great memories. They may be great people with great hearts, but great hearts don't always live by great philosophies and principles. It is also possible that 2 great people are moving in different directions in life.*
> *Find people who will challenge you, help you achieve your dreams and goals, and hold you accountable for your commitments. Find people who live by the philosophies and principles of a great life and those who can help you become the best version of yourself. This is one of the greatest success principles in life.*
>
> *PS: Success is different for us all but the principle applies to everyone.*
>
> *"It's your time to THRIVE"*
> —Michael Johnson - The Mojo Master
> Founder of the Academy of Mind and Motivation.

So there you go. The importance of friends and family can have a huge impact on us, either negatively or positively, depending on the situation. Those around you who step up and support you through the hardest times, they are your true tribe. Nourish those quality relationships and choose your tribe wisely.

Appearance:
The most important thing right now is to get up and get going for the day. How you look is not the focus. Keep it simple: be neat, clean, and dress appropriately for the occasion. Don't worry about anything else, because right now your energy is reserved for surviving the emotional turmoil you've been in and the massive turnaround you've just started to make!

> *"The more motivated you are towards the change, the more success you will have."*
> —Unknown

Research Positivity:
Positive quotes can lift your mood and remind you of what you are seeking. Self-help books are also valuable tools. It is highly recommended to look more deeply into the particular subject that you're having issues with. Choose the easiest option for you, whether it's reading, audio, or watching videos. Even pinning inspirational quotes from Pinterest can be inspiring, and fun! The more you can learn about who you want to be and how to move past each issue, the more empowered you will be!

Ignoring it hasn't got you anywhere. But by facing it directly and taking action you will be the master of your own transformation!

> *"I appreciate that I'm investing in myself. I'm respecting my needs."*
> —Coral Emerson

Affirmations:

Yes, affirmations really are quite powerful. Find a quote that inspires you or reminds you of what you want to achieve within yourself. Print off several copies. Place it everywhere and keep looking at it until you believe it!

When I was at my lowest ebb and working my way back to recovery, I had about a dozen little slips of paper with this written on it: *"I appreciate that I'm investing in myself. I'm respecting my needs."*

I typed them up in different fonts and fitted them all onto an A4 sheet of paper, printed the page, and cut it up so I had about 12 separate bits of paper. I then put them in a variety of places where I would see them daily: my bathroom mirror, above the toilet-roll holder, in the car, on my work desk, in my handbag, bedside drawer, all over the place!

I kept them there until the message actually sunk in. This wonderful quote simply reminds us to ask, "Is this an investment… in myself, my health, my life? Here and now, or in the future?"

Over time I took them away as I was growing stronger and living by my own creed. Each time I took one away was evidence of positive growth, and I happily recycled them by using the back as a shopping list. I've just kept a couple only. One is in a suitcase, so I get a pleasant surprise and gentle reminder each time I pull it out to use it. The other is in the bathroom drawer, tucked under a couple of products where I get a glimpse from time to time. It reminds me to check in on myself and make sure I'm still onto it. I am.

> *"Celebrate your life!*
> *Because what you have created and experienced –*
> *the good, the bad, and everything in between –*
> *is unique to you."*
> —Coral Emerson

Essential Oils:

Pure essential oils are extraordinary in offering support. They actually resonate with all 4 Elements of Heart, Mind, Body, and Soul; and trigger a primal connection to nature and the world around us. Good quality oils have many healing benefits, as they are directly derived from the plant, tree, grass, root, bark, fruit, or flower. The richest qualities of that plant are found in the oils, bringing the best that Mother Nature can give, ready to support and nurture you through the ups and downs. Pretty much anything you think of, there's an essential oil for it. It's quite incredible.

My journey with essential oils has grown over the last few years as I've come to realise how much they benefit my life, on so many levels.

Having an essential oil diffuser in the house is brilliant and highly recommended. It helps create a wonderful atmosphere. My diffuser has been having a major workout while writing this book, haha! Peppermint and Wild Orange is a favourite aroma during those times, as it's the perfect blend for focus, creativity, and motivation. Mmm, yum. I not only diffuse these essential oils, but I add them to recipes too! I love making raw Cacao Bliss Balls with either Peppermint or Orange oil. Now, do check carefully as only certain brands of essential oils are certified as edible and only certain oils can be ingested. Be sure to get a very high-quality essential oil, Certified Pure Therapeutic Grade or Certified Pure Tested Grade (CPTG), read the labels and information, and do your research.

Essential oils can also be used to minimise toxins in your home, and in your health and skincare regime. They can replace all the dreadful chemicals found in many products used around the house and on our bodies. Considering how much we absorb through our skin, a great way to bring the body back into balance is to go as natural as possible.

On an emotional level, during my most difficult times, I used a couple of carefully chosen essential oils to help bring some relief to my distressed emotional state. And they really did help when I was at my lowest ebb. Subtle but also very powerful, which is just what I needed at the time.

These days I use them for so many things: cooking, health, for relaxation and sleep, or to be focused and alert, freshen up the house, while working, pain relief, emotional support, natural cleaning, natural perfume and homemade body products, and simply to create a lovely aroma and set a positive uplifting mood.

I have every reason under the sun to love and enjoy essential oils!

If you're curious about which essential oils will benefit you, I will recommend some awesome ones at the end of each chapter that will help offer support. Each one has been chosen for its qualities that most suit that particular part of the journey; however, when it comes to essential oils, the best way to pick what you need is to be guided by what you feel attracted to at the time.

Disclaimer: Statements about essential oils and aromatherapy have not been evaluated by the Food and Drug Administration (FDA) or Therapeutic Goods Administration (TGA) or equivalent. The information shared is based on my own personal experience; however, it is for informational purposes only, and is not intended to be a professional medical diagnosis, opinion, or suggested course of treatment. Please consult with a qualified medical professional to address specific health concerns you might have.

Keep busy:

A job, volunteer work, or other positive activities, help immensely to take your mind off things. In the early stages of battling through everything, this is a life saver! While you're in a low phase, pour yourself into it! Sometimes "distracting" yourself is the only way through it at the time.

However, distraction is just a temporary fix. It helps us deal with challenges in the short term, but not for the long term, which is what we're addressing in this book. By all means, go ahead and do lots of distracting. I know I certainly did! But you must face what it is you're trying to avoid. Only then will the true healing occur. Your life will shift and change, positively and fast, once you decide to take the path of moving forward.

"Think Actively and Act Positively."
—Coral Emerson

Socially:

Take the brave step to get yourself out and about and go to some social events. They are brilliant at giving you something new and different to think about, plus an initial distraction with a long-term benefit. You can meet lots of interesting people with a tremendous variety of personalities. If nothing else, this can be amusing! But it is also very rewarding and helps you develop your confidence within yourself. It may even lift your spirits and make you want to smile. Even if it doesn't, at least you put yourself out there. Take it as a win!

There is no need to try to be anything you're not, just be yourself. We are all different, after all – and we all go through different phases in our lives. You won't be the only one at a social gathering who is going through "stuff."

Just get out there and say hello. The rest will follow.

> *"Find the light in your soul and you will always be blessed."*
> —Coral Emerson

Soul Connection:

Finding a deeper connection... in yourself, Mother Nature, The Universe, God, Buddha... whatever resonates with you most of all, will help to give you more strength. This important aspect to ourselves can be so easily forgotten in troubled times... and yet this is when we need to remember our soul connection the most. That divine connection to something far greater than what we can see in front of our eyes.

It's the "magic" that exists, whether we see it or not.

Getting in touch with nature, with your 'self', meditating, listening to inspiring music, being with others who share similar beliefs or have a positive outlook on life... all of these actions will help lift your soul energy. Also spend time with people who are motivating and inspirational in your life. If you don't know any, look for groups with similar interests to you, and you will find them.

Remember, you are more than just a body with thoughts and feelings...

You are: Heart, Mind, Body, *and* Soul.

Put it out to the Universe or your subconscious mind. Focus on your good intent and the energy going beyond you. If you are confused about what you need, the Universe or your higher self is confused too. It'll throw a lot of different things in your direction until you work it out.

So, get clear on your intentions and goals, on what you want to achieve, and move forward in that direction both by your own physical actions and the desire you create within your soul. A focused direction helps draw all the right energy into your life to make it happen.

I have found that one of the most interesting and unexpected aspects to a spiritual journey is actually a mental one: turning your life around by turning your thoughts around. I can highly recommend reading and researching, and sharing with like-minded people, as this will broaden your perception immensely.

Finances:

This might be the last thing you feel like thinking about... but let's start to get it sorted.

If money is not an issue to you, feel free to simply skip this bit, but just a gentle reminder to review your finances down the track to make sure everything is the best it can be. Your financial security is important at all stages of life.

If money (or the lack of it) is of great concern to you, and you're really in a pickle, firstly seek help from government or charitable agencies immediately, if they are available in your area. There is also a lot of information, online or in books, to assist you with financial planning or budgeting.

I'll be the first to admit that understanding money in great depth isn't my thing. It might not be yours either. But do you know what? There are plenty of other people out there who get it. So just for now, straighten yourself up, go down to your local bank branch, and take some time to talk to them about your account. Get them to check that everything is running as efficiently as possible.

You might find that in fact there are new accounts that suit your current situation better. I certainly did. There are many things that can be achieved in this one simple appointment: more interest, less fees, and (if you haven't already) set up a good savings system. It would be wise to consider taking out an affordable portion of your money from each pay day and placing it into another account specifically set up for saving. Also, if you're interested, ask for a referral for a good Financial Advisor to follow up on later. Some banks provide this as a free service for the first appointment, and you'll be surprised what you might pick up just from that one meeting.

Save 10% of your income, or whatever you're comfortable with, and put it aside… for you, for later, not to be touched! It will grow steadily and securely, and provide some financial support for your future. When the time comes, use it wisely.

If you're looking to improve your finances, I can highly recommend the following books:

The Barefoot Investor, by Scott Pape

Rich Dad Poor Dad, by Robert Kiyosaki

The Richest Man in Babylon, by George S Clason

Brilliant Budgets and Despicable Debt, by Heidi Farrelly

Mortgage Free, by Heidi Farrelly

Also look at other areas that can be improved, like insurance and phone bills, for example. A while back I contacted my phone provider and not only came away in credit for an error they'd made, but also managed to cut my phone bill almost in half by choosing a new and more suitable phone plan. Of course, I had to ring them to find all that out though. But it's worth investigating and contacting these types of companies directly to see if they can do any better, in an effort to keep their valued customer.

If you have no idea where your money is going or what you're spending it on, in the process of understanding your own finances, and while you're looking into it more deeply, keep all of your receipts. I mean ALL of them. If you've got no idea where it goes, you're about to find out. Don't be afraid of this – it can be a little unnerving at first, when you start to realise where it all gets distributed. But it's also quite revealing, and can be very helpful in creating healthier spending habits, which is only going to benefit you in the long run. You will achieve a lot more if you know your finances *and* have control over them.

If you're thinking, "But I don't have the money to do all of the things I want to," then you've just found a super important issue for you: finances, and the desire to improve them. Sorting your finances is your priority, alongside looking after your health and creating a positive mindset, of course.

Some things don't cost any money at all; ironically, the most important things. Also, if times are tough financially, don't let it stop you from all the positive changes you want to make. Focus on what you *can* do! This doesn't take money, what it does take is some dedicated time and your desire to put your energy into it.

So for now, start to think about how you would like to improve your finances, and most importantly, why? When you have a WHY you also have the motivation and the steering force behind the actions you need to take next.

> *"Dreams can come true, but only if you follow them."*
> —Coral Emerson

Write a list of financial goals. Achieving these will come later, but begin the thought process now. Make this fun; now is the time to think about that holiday you've always dreamed of. Write the list, and then come back to it later as you start to work towards your dreams and goals.

FINANCIAL GOALS:

- ....
- ....
- ....

> *"We don't need love to survive.*
> *We need love to thrive."*
> —Coral Emerson

Relationships:

I do not pause on relationships for long. Why? Well, because as important as they are, this is all about your relationship with yourself.

Whether you're in a relationship or single, either way this experience is just as important to you. It's still *your* journey. Whether you're sharing it with someone else or not – your journey is your journey, and the stronger you are and happier within yourself, the better it is for everyone around you anyway. It's a win-win situation.

If you are in a relationship that you feel needs improving, then put that on your list as a priority, and research the resources available to you to make the necessary changes. Taking action will always get a result.

Hopefully your life partner will support you in this. If not, it's up to you to be strong and do what you know in your heart to be right, to support your own dreams and desires no matter what anyone else thinks. A loving partner will be happy for you to be happy, simple as that.

> "The love that you withhold is
> the pain that you carry."
> —Ralph Waldo Emerson

Heartbreak? Well, I could write a whole book on it. In fact, that's what this book was going to be about, until I started writing it and realised it wasn't about that at all. In analysing my journey, it occurred to me the distress I was feeling during that time was much more multi-layered. So, if you're in the same situation, stay with me, this book is perfect for you!

One thing I will share with you... the reason I was so heartbroken is not only because of how much I loved this particular person, but also because I love so incredibly *deeply* in general. It is a part of my nature. I have come to accept that it is a gift. Where you find your true strength is in harnessing that energy and never letting anything stop the flow again. So LOVE! And never stop loving. It is indeed very powerful.

If you are single and struggling with the concept of being single, consider this: You need to bring out the best in you. Because if you don't, how can you expect anyone else to see it?

Being happy and confident in yourself, having fun and

loving life, not only means you're having a great life no matter what, but will naturally enhance your attractiveness and heighten your appeal to any potential partners. If you've created the life you want, or are at least on the path to it, and are a happy, confident person to be around, you will be irresistible to the right person. If it hasn't happened yet, either the right person hasn't appeared or you're not quite where you want to be in this place and time (so the right person can't even 'see' *the real you*).

I mean, if we haven't worked ourselves out and can't see our own true potential, we certainly can't expect someone else to see what a real gem we are underneath it all can we? Work on yourself first and enjoy this process! All else will follow as it should. When people love life, they're attractive right? Here's to the sexier, happier, healthier you.

Essentially, when it comes to relationships, the person who makes us happier than when we're happy on our own is the one to be with. Don't compromise for anything less.

> *"Be the love, and show the love, that you want to receive."*
>
> *– Coral Emerson*

I wanted to share something with you that I found recently on Instagram. It resonated deeply with me. Tough love at its best! I only wish I could've read this years ago, after dragging my sad and sorry heart through the mud for way too long. A personal choice... not a great one though! I'm all good now, but what I really needed was the harsh truth, and in a way that would impact me and leave its indelible mark. And that's what I found in these words below.

Maybe it's the perfect timing for you right now, perhaps it's exactly what you need to hear… breaking you free so you can release the heartbreak and move forward to something even better.

Although this is written in the perspective of the heartbreaker being male and the heartbroken being female, if that is not the case for you just change that bit as you read it.

It is the meaning in the words that is most important.

> *"If a man doesn't call you, it's because he doesn't want to call you. If he doesn't invite you to go outside it's because he doesn't want to see you. If he treats you like shit, it's because he doesn't care. If he lets you go, it's because he doesn't want to be with you. Don't keep playing his confusing games. Don't justify him.*
>
> *When a man says "I'm not ready but you're the love of my life and only one I want, but now is not the right time." It's simply because he doesn't want you. When a man wants to be with a woman, he stays with her without lies, excuses and complications.*
>
> *Stop being genuine and naive, and stop justifying his every excuse and every complication and put yourself first. You DO NOT need someone that doesn't know what they want, you DO NOT need someone that doesn't see your worth.*
>
> *Stop breaking your own heart for someone who probably won't even be as good as you expect, give yourself an opportunity to be happy and be with someone who actually deserves you.*
>
> *You deserve a man who knows your worth and fights for you every day."*
>
> —@thegoodwriters

You do deserve true love. I know it with all my heart!

> *"If your compassion does not include yourself,
> it is incomplete."*
> —Buddha

Overview:

Is this all sounding rather obvious? Like common sense? Perhaps you're thinking these recommendations are just a combination of normal, everyday things. Well, yes, *but are you doing them?* When we are in the thick of it, we let everything slip. It can be pretty hard to remember that we are important too. That we are the ones who need to pull ourselves back into line. Getting back to basics is the first step. Let's get these foundations strong – and we can build the awesome you that you always wanted to be!

The idea here really is to keep bringing it back to basics. Are you sleeping well? If not, that's your main focus. Next, what are you eating? Are you feeding your body the nutrition it needs? Make adjustments ASAP. It's time to put yourself, your body, your health first! It's about keeping it simple... look at general health. Make an appointment to see your GP and sort out whatever you can. If there are health conditions you are stuck with, look at solutions, so you can manage and cope with it better.

This book is not just about getting you "back on track," but taking you above and beyond. Withering away in the darkness has to end right now. You may get back to the way you were before, but if that was a mediocre lifestyle, without passion and fulfillment, and you felt like something was missing... then that is just not good enough. Is that why you were put on this planet?! No.

You are worth far more than that. To those around you. To yourself. To the world!

The gift inside you may be hidden... but it's time for it to come out.

My friend, we cannot live life waiting for when "everything is right" and all will be okay then. The likelihood is that even if that time comes, it is usually fleeting.

Everything is constantly evolving and changing and we cannot control the circumstances around us. We can only control how we react to it. So why wait? Why wait for this wonderful future that we're all eagerly anticipating? Many of us think to ourselves "Come on, hurry up, everything will feel better when this or that has happened." Instead, make it better *now*! Or at least take the actions and steps towards the direction of the kind of life that is better for *you*. There truly is no time like the present.

> *"The best parts of life are hiding in plain sight, embrace the ordinary and I promise you'll see them."*
> —Katherine Schafler

Let's open the door to the next stage. Ahead in Key 2 we'll look at one of the most important steps in this process – letting go. The more we hold on to things that aren't working for us, the less opportunity we have to progress forward into the future we desire. I can help make this process much easier for you. The benefits will be tremendous, because what comes after that is very exciting, but you must get through the next stage first, so that you're ready to be the you you've always wanted to be.

KEY POINTS
- Safety – top of the list, no doubt about it. Be safe!
- Fix it. Change it. Let it go – take this approach to help simplify everything
- Focus on a healthy and balanced lifestyle
- Sleep – a priority
- Good morning – set a good routine
- Activity – get movin' n groovin'
- Food – is thy medicine
- Mindset – turn negative thoughts into positive ones
- Look at the horizon – increase your scope of vision
- Talking – express your emotions in a safe environment so they can be dealt with
- Home – needs to be your sanctuary
- Family and Friends – embrace their support, reach out if you need to
- Appearance – make an effort if you can, but your inner well-being takes priority
- Read or research – be enlightened by other viewpoints and experiences
- Keep busy – this is essential during this stage
- Socially – start to add in some social events to begin exploring your happier side again
- Soul Connection – reflect on your deep beliefs and values
- Finances – take control, get advice, and do your best under the circumstances
- Relationships – treasure your relationship, but treasure yourself within the relationship too
- Be your own best friend – no one knows you better!

- Essential Oil support: cedarwood, lavender, lemon, peppermint

KEY ACTIONS

- [ ] Build a support network, write a list of people or services who you can turn to for help
- [ ] Realise what changes you want to make and write a list of issues you want to tackle
- [ ] Visit your doctor or a health professional to assist with any health concerns
- [ ] Support your body with nutritious food
- [ ] Write a list of financial goals
- [ ] Print off the quote "I appreciate that I'm investing in myself. I'm respecting my needs."
- [ ] Explore: Heart, Mind, Body, and Soul. These Elements make you who you are. And it's important that each of them is honoured in your life. Focus on balancing all 4 Elements.

"We cannot become what we want to be by remaining what we are."

—Max DePree

KEY 2

Release

Okay, so next we're going to look at what's holding you back. After you go through this process you will come out the other side refreshed and ready for the new you. Now that you have recognised the issues that you want to address, it's time to clear a path for that bright new future.

It is time to LET GO.

Let go of everything that's holding you back, everything that is simply not working for you anymore.

It's time for forgiveness, of yourself and others. All the frustrations, anxieties, fears, unrequited love, hurt, pain... any negative thought, feeling, sensation... none of these are aiding you on your life journey. When you realise you don't need to hold on to them anymore, you will be released from a heavy weight.

Holding on to it all is like lugging around a heavy old suitcase full of junk. During my journey, I've realised this: I've let go of the baggage... because baggage is no use to me. But luggage... well that's full of handy things that can be useful when you need them.

The important shift in mindset here is to not focus on what you're giving up, rather focus on what you have to *gain*! You have so much to gain by letting go... to open up to new experiences!

Now this is important: While you're on the path of release, keep up with the progress you're making from

Key 1. Continue the positive steps that you're taking there. To get the best results, don't stop until you resolve each of your major issues. Resolving issues requires a lot of release – it goes hand in hand.

What you will find as you start to let things go is that new aspects enter into your life. In the natural flow of 'release' there will be new opportunities and positive experiences to enjoy.

Letting go doesn't always mean you're giving up on something. Letting go means you can either "let it be," or that it no longer works for you.

The emotional release of letting go is going to be the most powerful and the most healing of all.

I highly recommend continuing with your counsellor, psychologist, life coach, mentor, support group or best friend, and really work through this with them. You will move ahead in leaps and bounds if you are willing to do this.

Is your mind feeling cluttered? It's time to find ways to relax, to resolve issues, to unburden your load in a safe environment.

Relationships? Do you feel loved, supported, safe, and enriched by your relationships with the people around you? Consider your family and friends as your tribe. Who would you want in your tribe? And who contributes to the tribe's overall well-being? To your well-being?

Is your living space doing your head in?! Then it's time to clean, clear, and cleanse. And make everything as fresh as possible so that you have the space to think clearly, and feel comfortable and healthy in your own space.

Your work area, does it have positive energy, a good vibe? Take a look around and see if there's anything you can contribute to improving your work environment.

Consider your body... are you feeling healthy? Or worn-out and way off track? Then eliminate what is bad for you and increase what is good for you. Spend some time working this out, as you will be generously rewarded for your efforts!

> *"Let it Go and Let it Flow."*
> —Coral Emerson

So, it's time to de-clutter your life, your mind, relationships with others, household items, your work area, even your body! Everything in your life that needs refreshing.

There are many books out there if you want to delve into this in a big way, as well as lots of information online with very helpful advice on de-cluttering (for *all* the different areas of your life).

Pick the most important area to start with and go for it! Then work your way through each one that is relevant to you.

Remember: *Change it, Fix it, Let it go* - this applies to everything, from material items, to emotional, mental, physical, and spiritual. It could be health, wealth, relationships, friendships, career, location. Apply the *Change it, Fix it, Let it go* strategy to all the different aspects of your life and it will quickly free you up for a more positive future.

One of my favourites (and something that can be done regularly) is to sort out my living space. Honestly, the clearer it is, the clearer my mind! I don't want a mind that's full of clutter or junk. I want it to be free of all that, to allow all the good stuff to flow through.

If you also want to clear the mess out of your mind, then it's time to clean the mess out of your life! So here are some tips I'd like to share with you.

"Does it spark joy?"
—Marie Kondo

De-clutter your living space:

This is a great time for the release of unwanted items. Getting rid of the clutter will help to clear your mind. It seems we can drag a lot of junk around with us, not just in our head and heart, but in our house! Truly, do you really need *all* of it? Really?

Believe me, sorting out all this practical stuff will do you the world of good.

If you're carrying around anything that isn't practical and doesn't make you feel wonderful, then it has no use in your life. Wow – how does that feel? Like a huge weight lifted off your shoulders?

When letting go of materialistic items and wondering what to do with them next, consider the following options:

1. Sell it
2. Gift it
3. Charity
4. Upcycle
5. Recycle

One of the most common and frustrating clutter issues people have, is paperwork… groan…

Okay, so it's time to sort through it. Get rid of anything that you no longer need. Along the way you may find some things that need attention. Put them aside in your

"To Do" pile and sort them out according to priority.

Remember to shred any old personal documents that are no longer required. Also, check the time limit for important or business-related documents that may need to be kept for a certain number of years.

An example of the most common paperwork issues that arise are:

Taxation

If you're all up-to-date, great, you can start preparing for the next financial year. If not, then don't hesitate any longer. You want to clear the slate. Start afresh. This will need to be done on all levels, including something as mundane as taxes - apologies to the accountants out there!.

Superannuation

Make sure you have the best super account for yourself, and very importantly, roll-over *all* your funds into one. Don't wait any longer on this one! The amount of fees chewing up your money when it's all spread around in separate accounts... well, you don't even want to know! This is actually a very quick and simple process. I can't believe how long I put this off, I could kick myself. Contact all your superannuation companies, and also the Taxation Department, to make sure you've found all of your super. Merge it as quickly as you can.

Filing

It's time to get the filing system in order, so that you can find everything when you need it, and important papers and processes don't get lost or left unfinished.

This will help tremendously in efficiency and in finally feeling organised. Once you've done it properly it's very easy to continue with, and will save you heaps of time. Time better spent doing other things.

Financial Advice:

Right, it's time to look deeper into your financial situation. You may like to consider a financial advisor. Or, if having a dedicated advisor doesn't fit into the budget, or is not your kind of thing, then perhaps seek out someone you know who is successful in managing their finances and ask for their assistance and advice. Whatever monetary status we're in, we can usually do better. That's what your advisor or mentor is there for. Make the most of it – this is an investment in your financial security. Show them the list of your financial desires, be open about your financial situation, and go from there.

Commitments:

Ask yourself, "Is it right for you, right now?" This could be sports, a hobby, any group or extra-curricular activity. Even if you've loved it before, it doesn't always mean it's beneficial to your life right now. Consider what you might like to let go of, and just as importantly in this instance, what you want to keep dedicating your time and energy to.

For me, I found that my involvement in local theatre no longer resonated with me, whereas it once used to be a really important part of my life. I'd been on stage for over 20 years… but it didn't mean I had to keep doing it. I realised I simply didn't have the time or energy for it any more, my health was making it challenging and I couldn't give the commitment required, and it's important to me that I fulfil my commitments. I realised I needed that space to allow other new experiences into my life. I still love theatre, and maybe one day I will tread the boards again.

> *"Everything you are going through is preparing you for what's next."*
> —Kerwin Rae

When challenges close doors, they open new ones:

When I was diagnosed with **FND** (Functional Neurological Disorder), it changed my life. There was relief in finally getting an answer, but there was also a lot of worry about what the future looked like.

My high-pressure job was no longer going to be viable. My doctor strongly suggested I step away and allow myself some recovery time. The only thing is, I knew that as soon as I left that position, I would never be able to get a "regular" job again. Due to my health and the challenges the condition presented; I was fully aware I had become unemployable.

I've always been very independent, so this did not sit well with me. But reality set in and I simply had to do what was right for my health.

FND is more common than we realise. It can be as debilitating as Multiple Sclerosis and Parkinson's disease, and may present with similar symptoms. Unfortunately, it does not have the support or resources that a lot of other neurological conditions have. It can also be a slow and frustrating process to get diagnosed.

Physical symptoms of FND may include the following:

- Seizures
- Muscle weakness
- Partial or complete paralysis
- Partial or complete loss of sensation
- Gait and balance problems
- Involuntary movements
- Difficulty reading and writing
- Difficulty speaking
- Poor cognitive abilities
- Unexplained pain
- Decreased alertness
- Extreme fatigue

The symptoms put myself, and my employer, in a very difficult position. It was time to go.

After allowing myself some time to recuperate, I knew I had to make an important decision about my future. I was handed a disability form and started filling it out. But suddenly I was gripped by a vision of what my future might look like, and it wasn't heading in the direction I wanted.

I tore up the form and threw it into the fireplace! A somewhat cathartic experience looking back on it now. I made a significant decision right there and then, that I was going to take control of the situation and find a way to make it work, despite the challenges.

My aim was to turn my disability into an "ability", remain independent and find the strengths that I still had left within me to create positive change in my life and others. With an attitude of "Focus on what I can do, rather than what I can't."

I had a business idea that I thought would suit my predicament, allowing me to help others (something I love to do), remain independent and have the flexibility I needed to look after my health.

This was a huge turning point, where one of my greatest challenges became the impetus for a positive step in the right direction for my life and a future that I could now look forward to.

The condition may take away control of my own body when an episode hits, but I realised I could take control of everything else. It was a pathway I might not have seen, had I not had the *need* to seek it.

Because of this, I am grateful. It is not an easy path, I'm certainly up against a few hurdles. But the journey was meant for me for some reason. Just like yours is meant for you. And it's up to you what you decide to do with it.

Tap into what you *can* do and see what direction it takes you. Let those challenges open your eyes, and open doors, to new opportunities.

> *"To be yourself in a world that is constantly trying to make you something else, is the greatest accomplishment."*
> —Ralph Waldo Emerson

Pleasant Events Schedule:

This is the best! What an eye-opener!

Do you want to work out what it really is that gets you going? In a good way, haha. I discovered this really awesome tool, the *Pleasant Events Schedule*. It makes you very aware of what you do and don't like doing, and how often these activities are done. People will usually discover that they are occupying themselves with things that they'd rather not be doing (and spending a long time doing it), and hardly ever spending any time doing what they would love to be doing!!! Perhaps haven't even done for years!

A prime example for me: When I was a child, I loved riding my push bike. And yet I stopped riding bikes as an adult. I thought, "Well, why wouldn't I still enjoy this activity?" So, I went and invested in a cool mountain bike. I was a bit apprehensive at first as my attempts to ride again could be described as hilarious!! But I persisted and in a short space of time it quite literally was like "getting back on the bike."

My life blossomed from this one decision. The feeling of the wind in my hair, the sense of freedom, the challenges of corners and bumpy bits on the path, plus my fitness improved and I get outdoors more. It's also something I can enjoy on my own or with company, which is great as I'm not reliant on anyone else to get out there and have fun, but of course the fun can be increased with a friend!

If you want to step back and take a good look at your life, at the things that fill it up, I highly recommend going ahead and doing the *Pleasant Events Schedule*. It only takes a few minutes, but it sure does open your mind!

For me this was a HUGE turning point and revelation.

To check out the *Pleasant Events Schedule*, please head to the back of the book for the link.

Self-talk:

Be aware of negative self-talk and change it – this very instant.

Understandably, there are many instances where forgiveness can be extremely difficult, particularly if you need to resolve something with someone who has passed on, or who you won't see again. In those situations, it will be necessary to resolve it in yourself, so that you can heal. If you can heal, you can also grow strong. You owe it to yourself to heal yourself of the pain in your soul wherever possible. Holding onto anger, sadness, or any other negative feeling is actually really hurting you. You are the one who has to deal with those feelings, which means you are the one suffering. It doesn't mean that past hurts will be forgotten, but what it does mean is that you're willing to let go of that pain so it no longer damages you or controls you anymore, allowing you to learn from the experience and move on in your life. Forgiveness truly is an incredible tool to ultimate release and peace.

Even a fleeting moment of feeling forgiveness is incredibly empowering! Everyone has the capacity to forgive. And everyone has the capacity to change. Look into your heart and see how you can shift this blockage and bring peace back into your life.

I remember an unusual experience which involved forgiveness...

A few years ago I was struggling with heartbreak from a brief, but deeply passionate, romantic connection. I was shattered and it was taking me a long time to come to terms with it, much longer than I ever thought it would take. While I was still resolving this in myself, I met someone nice, and we decided we'd like to start a new relationship. Deep down though, I knew I had to overcome the heart-wrenching feelings I still had lingering within me, so that I could honour my new partner. It was time to forgive. But oh my goodness, I wasn't sure how on earth I would do that. I sat down on the floor in front of my bookshelf, pondering this very thought. I went with my intuition and pulled out a little book called *Perfect Calm* by Alan Hewitt. I opened it up randomly and my eyes fell upon this page:

> *"ALWAYS FORGIVE: Free yourself now by forgiving others you believe have let you down. Holding onto feelings of bitterness and disappointment can be more damaging to you than those you direct them at."*
> —Alan Hewitt

> *"To forgive is the highest, most beautiful form of love. In return you will receive untold peace and happiness"*
> —Robert Muller

I read those words, tears streaming down my face, my thoughts went to this person in my past, and I said out loud, "I forgive you." It was an incredible moment, it felt like my heart expanded, and a weight lifted off my shoulders… I felt free! Yet it was only a few seconds, that's all it took. Once you feel it, you *feel* it! And it's one of the best feelings ever.

What was even more magical about this experience was what came next…

A few weeks before this I'd lost the necklace given to me by this person. It was a beautiful piece of jewellery and I still loved it regardless. I'd looked *everywhere* for it. Now I don't usually lose things, so this was unusual for me. Coming back to my moment of forgiveness, wiping the tears off my face and feeling like a new woman, I leaned over to the bookcase to put the book back. There, right at the back of where I was about to put the book, was something sparkling! Yes, it was the necklace!! Wow! I was blown away at the synchronicity of it all. It fully emphasised how forgiveness is such an incredible gift.

> *"The key to being happy is knowing you have the power to choose what to accept and what to let go."*
> —Dodinsky

Clinical Hypnotherapy:

Ready to break some bad habits or improve your well-being? A lot of things can be helped along with hypnotherapy, which could range from quitting smoking, assistance with weight loss, negative thought patterns, stress, anxiety, heartbreak, fears, and much more. Imagine if these strong emotions and sensations and/or addictions didn't control you anymore. Feel the freedom of changing negative thinking, reactions and behaviours.

I highly recommend this as a brilliant way to support the changes you're going through. I personally found it very helpful in supporting all the other things I was doing at the time. This is the ideal stage to begin this process now to help get you through this difficult time and continue with it until you see results. Usually not many sessions are needed and it's quite quick, but don't give up if it isn't. The results will vary for each person and for each issue that needs addressing, but it's definitely worth trying.

This is a very powerful aid on the journey to self-improvement. The most important changes we can make are those within ourselves. The beauty of hypnotherapy is that it can gently reach the subconscious... the part that controls a lot of what we do but leaves us wondering why!

Make sure you choose a professional clinical hypnotherapist by getting a referral from your local health professional, or a recommendation from a good friend if they've had positive results from someone in particular. And then trust in the process. As well as enjoy a bit of quiet time out for yourself! The effect after a session is subtle yet strong, and it has the potential to help immensely.

I personally found this method aided in strengthening what I was already working on, particularly when I needed a bit of extra help.

Hypnotherapy can be used for many things. It is typically known for helping with unhealthy habits and addictions. But it can also be used to build confidence and a positive mindset. It's especially effective in all aspects of letting go and releasing any unwanted thought patterns and behaviours.

Other health professionals:

If you haven't done so already, it would be wise to start booking appointments with other health professionals who can take you further in your search for better health, focusing on the areas you specifically need support with. Also consider professionals who work with alternative therapies, as this will considerably increase the options to help alleviate health issues and most importantly find the right balance for you.

This could be as diverse as:

Physiotherapist, chiropractor, osteopath, nutritionist, optometrist, podiatrist, skin specialist, naturopath, Bowen therapy, Reiki, meditation, spiritual healing, Aromatouch Technique, kinesiology, pain management specialist, gym or personal exercise program, yoga, Pilates, acupuncture, therapeutic massage, etc.

Look at what your highest needs are right now and start resolving them one by one. Focusing your attention on this area of your life is a strong indicator that you are honouring your body and dedicated to improving your well-being. Taking this action alone will help to increase a positive mindset and a more hopeful outlook for the future.

> *"The fact that you're doing something positive, is positive!"*
> —Coral Emerson

Appearance:

When times get tough, sometimes we can let things slip. Making a little extra effort, to take care of how you look can have a tremendous ability to lift self-esteem.

Start doing more things for yourself, for your body, that make you look and feel good. The point of this is not so much about appearance, but rather about how it makes you feel to put in extra effort, by gently nudging yourself out of the comfort zone you're in right now. Every single thing you do to honour yourself, no matter how small, makes a difference.

Consider if there are any changes you might like to make, or pampering you'd like to enjoy to perk yourself up again? Make a note of these, because the mini-makeover is coming up soon!

> *"Don't be afraid to go out on a limb. That's where the fruit is."*
> —Jackson Browne

Confidence:

As you let go of the old, it is important to have confidence in what you are doing and in what you wish to achieve. Search for techniques to learn about self-confidence. This can be done many ways: attending a course or workshop, reading about the subject, discussing this with a health professional, asking others who have the kind of confidence you're seeking what their secret is. If you want to learn about something, you need to study it and practice it. Treat confidence in this way and it will come to you too.

Hey, I'll admit I'm not always confident. I have to work at it! In fact, I'm more of an introvert than extrovert, and can be quite shy at times. From my experience, any step forward in increasing confidence, even just a little step, makes a big difference to stepping forward into life in general.

Believe it or not "Fake it till you make it" can actually be useful. Simply *act* like someone who is confident... and then - ta-dah!! - before you know it you actually feel more confident. This is just a quick solution of course, and a temporary one, but it really can help.

I tested this theory out many years ago. As a shy 15-year-old I didn't know how others were so confident. I was curious to see what would happen if I pretended to be confident. I couldn't believe it; it was like a mirror of confidence reflecting outwards and having it shine back at me. After that I wasn't quite so shy anymore; well, at least not all the time, anyway. I've had to pull on this a few occasions throughout my life just to get through awkward situations, and it works every time. The wonderful thing is that over time it starts to feel more natural. Although you may feel like you are "pretending", it's simply just a technique to tap into a part of you that you're not familiar with, growing that confidence muscle, just like we need to with anything that's new and unfamiliar to us.

Confidence is an essential step to positive progress. And do you know what? The best thing of all is you can fool *yourself* with this trick. Taking back control and strengthening your mindset and reactions, you'll likely find you can start adding a bit more "pizazz and play" back into your life, and making some pretty awesome decisions. How fun does that sound?!

The "fake it till you make it" idea really is a light-hearted way to give this a go, but to step up to a whole new level, I love this adage from Jeff Goins: "We don't fake it till we make it. We believe it till we become it. And it takes the right environment and the right people to help make that happen." Absolutely brilliant!

The most important thing of course, is that you are still *you*. It's not about pretending to be someone else; it's about bringing that more confident part of yourself to the forefront when necessary. Confidence doesn't have to be loud – you can be quietly confident if that's more in your nature. It's mostly defined by working out *who* you are and *what* you're all about, and being comfortable with that. That sort of confidence is the most alluring.

> *"Be the Sunshine in Your Own Life!"*
> —Coral Emerson

Smile:

Even if you don't feel like smiling right now, I'm going to throw in a little experiment for you.

Whatever you're going through at the moment, just put it aside for now and think about the things that *normally* make you smile. Is it funny movies, a comedy show, walking in nature, seeing the sunset, watching bloopers, a hilarious friend, cute puppies, visiting a special place, volunteering, being involved in an interest or hobby?

Write down all of the things that put a smile on your dial, and put the list in a place where you can see it regularly. Even better, find images of the things that make you smile, and create a 'Smile' album. Choose whatever format you like best, whether it's on the computer, in your phone, or in a scrapbook or folder. Wherever is easy for you to find it and look at it.

So anytime you need a pick-me-up, go to your album or list, and look at the images or words to help lift your spirit and put a smile on your face.

I'm a total sucker for Corgis! You know that thing they do, when they lay flat on the ground and their little legs stick out? It's just the cutest! Yep, I have a big goofy smile right now!

Treat yourself:

Take time out to be with yourself, take yourself somewhere special, or reward yourself with a wonderful gift. Yes – just for you! Remember, gifts can come in many packages: doing something you love, being with people you love, or buying something nice for yourself.

It might be as simple as listening to your favourite music, lighting a candle, going for a walk in the park, forest, or along the beach, perhaps taking a little holiday, whale watching, having a relaxing massage, going to concerts and events, having a cuppa with friends, riding a motorbike, reading a book, skydiving, photographing flowers in your garden, doing a jigsaw, watching a sunset. Whatever is positive and uplifting to you, is what you need to do! Best of all it brings a richness to your life because you are doing more, getting out and about, and exploring. Aim to achieve at least one of these special rewards to yourself regularly.

Write down the rewards you look forward to most of all. Pick one for now and know that you can do the others any time that you are ready.

My rewards:

- ....
- ....
- ....

You will benefit from it in many ways. First of all, and most importantly, you've decided that you are worth it! Now that is a huge achievement!

One of the lessons you learn from this is to value yourself. The higher the value you place on yourself, the higher others will value you too. And the more enriched your life will become.

> *"Happiness is not the absence of problems, but the ability to deal with them."*
> —Charles de Montesquieu

Overview:

During the process of letting go, review what you want to keep in your life. Never let what's happened in the past ruin what you want to happen in your future.

Once you start bringing new things into your life, which is part of the journey you're on right now, something old just has to go! So, do you want *new* experiences? Well, let something go!!

Amazingly, you will start to find the time and space for something new in your life: YOU!

Coming up in Chapter 3, we will look at how to rebuild the life that you want, how to rebuild yourself, knowing that you now have the foundations set. All your hard work is about to pay off. This will be an incredible time of growth. Great things are to come!

KEY POINTS

- Continue with any Key Points and Actions from Key 1 that are relevant
- Commitments – are you taking on too much?
- Self-talk – make it positive
- Responsibility – you are responsible for yourself and your life
- Forgiveness – allow this tremendous gift to yourself
- Hypnotherapy – to help with the letting go process
- Health professionals – continue working through health issues
- Appearance – take good care of yourself
- Confidence – give it a boost
- Essential Oil support: frankincense, geranium, juniper berry, lemongrass

KEY ACTIONS

☐ Make a list of what you need to "let go"
☐ Dedicate time to the letting-go process – seek assistance if you need to
☐ Get financial advice or spend time organising your finances

- [ ] De-clutter your life on every level – yep, everything!
- [ ] Complete the Pleasant Events Schedule – link at the back of the book
- [ ] Create a 'Smile' list or album
- [ ] Plan a treat to celebrate your achievement on letting go and being ready to move on!
- [ ] Remember: In the Release stage, check that you are covering all aspects of Heart, Mind, Body, and Soul.

"Where does your heart go? Follow it."
—Coral Emerson

KEY 3

Rebuild

This is the fun bit! It's time to rebuild the life you want. This is where you get to be the director of your own production – your life. Where the doors are opening to your success and you're ready to step through them. You decide where you want to go, and point yourself in the right direction!

Find yourself:

While you are in the rebuilding stage it is good to step back and check on your progress.

- Are you heading in the direction you want to?
- Are you representing yourself in the manner you want to?
- Are you respecting yourself and your true motivations in life?
- Are you looking after **Heart**, **Mind**, **Body**, and **Soul**?

Make sure you're on track, because you want your precious energy to be going where it's needed the most.

If any old baggage comes up, remember this: it's *baggage*! Not useful. Transform it into luggage so that it can be useful, or, chuck it out of the suitcase altogether. If you don't need it, don't drag it along with you.

You will find as you travel this journey that the need

to release and let go is essential to the process of rebuilding. The more often you do it, the easier it is to keep on track with the rebuilding phase. Leave things in the past. *Learn* from the past, yes, but leave them in the past. So, while you're rebuilding, keep letting go of anything that's not necessary to you. Turn your focus to starting the exciting process of being who you really are! You are an amazing individual – it's time to embrace your awesomeness and to reach out for everything else you want to bring into your life.

> *"If you think you can do a thing, or you think you can't do a thing, you're always right."*
> —Henry Ford

Health:

It is incredibly important to keep on top of any health issues and continue to work towards your health goals. It was around this stage for me that I finally organised to have a proper skin cancer check... and yes, something was found, something that previous doctors had missed or dismissed. It was a basal cell carcinoma, which thankfully was easily and safely removed. I can tell you, I was very glad to get it out!

Keep progressing with resolving any issues that have come up for you in the stages of **Realise** and **Release**, and start to have fun now on the path to **Rebuild**!

> *"Happiness is the highest form of health."*
> —Dalai Lama

Happiness:

Ahh... the ever-elusive happiness! When happiness eludes us, it is not an *outside* something, it is an *inside* something. Yes, happiness can certainly be found on the outside, there are many situations that can bring us a lot of joy, but it is fleeting. These things come and pass, as does everything. They change, just as the scenery changes around us. But happiness on the inside is *always* with us! We just have to look for it, and create it! So, snap out of the unhappy and bring the bliss back into your life.

This doesn't always come easily, or naturally, but it's well worth the effort. Personally, I found that by **realising** what I needed to work on and minimising the effects of issues and addressing them head-on… by **releasing** unwanted junk out of my life and clearing away the effects of the past… by **rebuilding** who I want to be and the life I want to live… and by **refining** my life choices each day, I have found happiness in a more fulfilling and wholesome way than ever before. And it's not just temporary, it's for life!

As much as possible, choose happiness, or at least the things that contribute to your happiness. Simply choosing happiness is sometimes not always that easy. Hey, I get it; I go through that challenge too. At least if we're thinking about how to get that happy feeling back, we can also start to think about what brings us that wonderful sensation. I've noticed it's often a whole bunch of small choices and positive action combined, that reward us with those warm, fuzzy, happy feelings.

If you're really, really stuck, call your best buddy and talk it out. Just chatting to them, no matter what the conversation ends up being about, will help realign you. Talking to someone you love is just the best.

If you learn to tune in to your true self, you will find greater happiness than ever before. It's bursting to be let loose; in fact, it can't wait to get out of you! So open those doors and let it!

> *"For beautiful eyes, look for the good in others; for beautiful lips, speak only words of kindness; and for poise, walk with the knowledge that you are never alone."*
>
> —Audrey Hepburn

Mini-makeover:

The importance of how you look is relevant in how you feel.

This is not about beauty – or the *perceived ideas* of beauty – rather it is finding the best of you. Putting your best assets forward, so to speak.

Consider: *Heart, Mind, Body,* and *Soul.*

This rather playful section helps to bring it all together.

For now, we are concentrating on the body and the visual aspect to how you present yourself, as it has a lot of bearing on your confidence.

I've had an interesting insight into this, both in my personal life and career. I used to be a professional make-up artist and had the pleasure of working alongside award-winning photographers, in one of the largest studios in the city of Perth, Western Australia. During that time, I noticed a close link to how a person's physical appearance affected their mood. Clients would come in feeling (and looking) tired, run down, uncertain, reserved and low in confidence. With a bit of pampering, some quality time just for themselves, combined with grooming (hair, make-up, clothing and accessories), plus the fun vibe of a professional photo shoot; time and time again I observed dramatic changes to their mood, even a whole other side to their personalities!

Often when we let life drag us down, it affects our

looks. Generally, we lose our glow, our sparkle... and we look, and feel, tired and dull.

Well, it happened to me too. Comfortable clothes were my go-to (okay, okay, I'll admit it, I still love my comfy clothes!). I felt so drab, and sad, I really didn't want to look in the mirror. However, as I grew stronger and could feel that glow inside of me start to shine, I really wanted to shine on the outside too. It's just that my exterior hadn't quite caught up with my interior.

So, to celebrate the "new" me and to show myself appreciation for the hard work I'd put in to make these significant and long-lasting changes, I decided to plan a mini-makeover for myself. Once I'd made that decision, I discovered that I was actually looking forward to it. I had something planned that was going to be fun, with a positive outcome. Winning combination!

I was really starting to feel happier and healthier; therefore, I also wanted to *look* happy and healthy.

Consider this from another perspective... when we don't feel happy and healthy, and we want to, it sure helps when we look like we do. Hey, it's a trick we play on ourselves sometimes, but if it has great results, then so be it.

The reflection that you look at, is a reflection of yourself. You want this awesome NEW YOU to show on the outside too! Imagine a glowing, happy face shining back at you in the mirror. It's an instant confidence lift! And we all know how vital that is to positive personal growth.

Now look, if this is just not your thing, no worries at all. You just do you, my friend! I'm recommending it because it made a huge difference for me, and I have seen similar results in other people. I know that it helps, but what's most important of all, is that you do what's comfortable for you.

If you're on board with it and want to give it a go, the following is a good basis for a mini-makeover. However, choose only what feels right for you. The more you can do, the greater the transformation. The process is similar to the preparation for a very special occasion, like a wedding, school formal, or important presentation. Except that this time the important occasion isn't an occasion at all, it's just for you, to reward yourself. It's all about thanking yourself and stepping forward into this new chapter in your life, to celebrate how far you've come on your journey.

It is very important that you do this in a way that feels comfortable to you. Below are some ideas that can help direct you, but please alter it to suit yourself.

Mini-makeover – a few ideas to get you started:
- New hair-do
- Moisturise daily
- Eyebrow shaping
- Facial hair groomed
- Hair removal where desired
- Nails neat and clean
- Eyelashes and eyebrows tinted
- Makeup to enhance your best features

Add in your own ideas here:

- ....
- ....
- ....

...and then of course what you wear...

> *"Doing some work on your personal style is often a first attempt or a soft launch at personal development and self-reflection."*
> —Ciara Lowe-Thiedeman – The Style Counsellor

Clothes maketh the magic:

Take time to consider "the new you." What do you wear? Or more importantly what does the new you wear? How do you want to represent yourself from now on? Consider what type of clothes you actually need (i.e., work, social life, home life, hobbies and interests). Don't forget to upgrade your shoes and accessories too, if need be, to complement your new style.

Please note: If this is stretching it on your budget, and I know the feeling, then make the best of what you have and what you can find within your own wardrobe. Ask an honest friend for advice, to help you get rid of what simply doesn't work for you and concentrate on the items that do. Having another set of eyes on the contents of your wardrobe can be really handy.

Charity shops often have excellent options, just go in with a list of specific items that you require (otherwise it's easy to get carried away and come back with more things that you don't really need). Also, you don't want to fall back into the trap of buying the same old stuff (it happens automatically, it's normal). So, if you can, take that trusted friend along with you and they will keep you on track.

Every time I feel like having a wardrobe clear-out, I get my daughter to help me. There's nothing like a daughter's blunt honesty to really get things moving, haha!

If you get stuck, and want to make significant changes, then perhaps seek assistance from professionals in each field. Stylist, hairdresser, beautician, colour consultant, there's someone out there who does this for a living. The beauty of this is they can step back and look at the overall picture – you – with fresh eyes. Or you can even call upon your friends to help you look at yourself in a whole new way. If you admire someone else's style or dress sense, then they will be the perfect person to talk to. I'm sure you'll find that they will be thrilled to help. After all, it's the greatest compliment to them.

Going ahead with your mini-makeover will really cement all the hard work you've been doing for yourself recently. It is not only a reward for you, but it helps to create a far deeper transformation. When you can *see* a change, it truly is easier to believe the change. It will assist you in keeping up your strength and desire for continued improvement. Most importantly of all, you have acknowledged that you deserve it!

Special Treats:

Now that you're looking more like how you're feeling, remember to keep up the good work. Don't deny yourself some lovely treatments from time to time. You could include massage, pedicure, reflexology, facial, holistic healing, going on a retreat... whatever makes you feel great! By doing this for yourself you're saying, "I'm worth it."

If you're on a budget, then simply swap with a friend and give each other a bit of pamper time.

Make a list of some nourishing treatments or experiences that you would like to receive:

- ....

- ....

- ....

Discovering the sexy new you:

The sexiest thing about you is: YOU!

Yes, I'm sorry there's no great secret here! When you go to the effort of being the best version of yourself, of living life with love and passion, openly sharing your heart, following your dreams, honouring yourself and others… this is incredibly sexy.

I certainly feel this way and know those around me do too. To get a broader picture on this concept I asked a wide range of people from all different backgrounds, ages, gender identity, and sexual preferences. I asked them: "What do you find sexy?"

These are the answers I received:

- Compassionate
- Confidence
- Strength of character
- Honesty
- Morals
- Respect
- Intelligence
- Sense of humour
- Integrity
- Spontaneity
- Quirkiness
- Ability to hold a great conversation
- Their laugh
- A woman in her own power
- Smile
- Sparkle in their eyes

- Curious nature
- Acceptance
- Adventurous spirit
- Cheeky smile with a glint in her eye
- Authentic
- Passionate
- Kind
- Kindness to animals
- Modest
- Free spirit
- Dancing
- Genuine
- Selfless
- Nice eyes
- Fun
- Loyal
- Vivacious

Many of the qualities mentioned above were repeated several times by different people, in particular compassion, confidence, strength, honesty, good conversation, laugh and smile.

Did they mention any physical qualities, like certain body parts? For sure, I received some of those answers, but very few, and always accompanied with attractive personality traits too.

The information I received was very clear evidence that although we do have certain physical attributes that we're attracted to, it was an outstanding win that your sexiness comes from *who* you are as a person.

Ponder on that... think about the times you may have

held back because you might've been worried about how you looked, or what you were wearing. Then look at that list above... I bet you've got a heap of those qualities!

Yes, we have just recently covered the topic of how appearances can affect how you feel. Let me emphasis here... how *you* feel.

Feeling good about how you look is about your own inner confidence; it's not always about the layer of clothing you have on. What you wear, how you present yourself, can definitely make *you* feel good. How others perceive you, well that's up to them. But the ones that are worth it, will see beyond the external. If they've only just met you, the outside layer might catch their eye, but the inside flame will capture their heart.

I will admit that some of my "sexiest times" have occurred when I've been in my comfy old dressing gown or around-the-house clothes. It's all about what's underneath right! And how you feel about yourself and the energy you exude. At those times I was feeling completely comfortable, and completely *me*. And of course, in the presence of someone I love, who loved me in return.

But there have been situations where attraction comes unexpectedly and with a complete stranger. I can remember a couple of times where it certainly had nothing to do how I was looking.

A few years ago, at work, I was not wearing anything special I can tell you, and a guy walked in, tall, handsome, super gorgeous. Anyway, we got chatting. He had just returned from military service. Well, I have the deepest respect for those that serve, so I came out from behind the counter and gave him a big hug and said "Thank you". He knew exactly what I meant. I went back behind the counter, and he said he would love another one of those hugs. I walked out again, only to be picked up and spun around the room in a great big bear hug! It was an embrace that brought nostalgic visions of those romantic black and white photos from the 1940's. It was a simple moment, but a memorable one. I was glowing all over after that! It was such a nice feeling to know we – two complete strangers – had just made each other's day in a meaningful way.

Another time, back in the 90's, I caught the eye of a famous rockstar (no, I'm not going to reveal who it was). I was wearing a t-shirt and jeans at the time, and not even the sexiest version! It was all in the eyes… the vibe… he was fully immersed in his element (being on stage) and I was fully immersed in the music and his energy. There was something incredibly magnetic about it all. After the show he sought me out, pulled me to him in an intimate embrace and kissed me passionately. The sexual energy was so intense it could've blown the roof off! But we left it there… the intensity lingering in the air…

Remember, the sexiest thing about you, is YOU!

Focus my gorgeous friend, on the *you* that you want to be, and you will be oh so sexy!

> *"Getting my groove on!"*
> —Coral Emerson

Social life:

How's your social life looking? Are you getting out and about, meeting new people, as well as spending quality time with your friends?

It's time to branch out! If you start doing more and going to more events, you will find that life gets a zing to it!

Your experiences increase, your repertoire of making memorable moments becomes stronger than ever, and you will enjoy yourself!

Now I acknowledge this because I've been in this position… I understand there can be challenges. If health issues, finances, or time are a factor, then choose how you spend your social time wisely. It's more about *quality* than quantity anyway.

Push past the comfort zone, because the benefits will far outweigh any initial hesitation. Think about it… you'll have more to talk about for starters, therefore conversations will flow more easily as you'll have a bigger range of things to talk about, which means that life has become more interesting too!! How about that! Pretty good pay-off, hey?

Opposites attract:

Try something NEW.

This can be fun, but challenging at times too. During this stage, I decided to start doing the opposite of what I normally do!

Things I'd usually say "Yes" to, I said "No" to (unless, of course, I actually really did love doing them).

Conversely, the things I would normally say "No" to, I considered saying "Yes" to!

So, if you're up for the challenge and to try out something new, I highly recommend giving it a go. This, of course, must sit comfortably within your own personal moral standards and values, and with a consideration for safety at all times.

What you're trying to achieve here is a NEW way of thinking and of challenging yourself. By bringing a new energy into your life and changing what you "normally" do, you ultimately open doors to new aspects of yourself and your life. When you start doing that, everything around you will start changing too. And isn't that what you're aiming for?

> *"We keep moving forward, opening new doors, and doing new things, because we're curious and curiosity keeps leading us down new paths."*
> —Walt Disney

Career:

Love it or leave it! Not immediately, of course! There are bills to be paid right. But if your job is a major contributing factor to your unhappiness, causing health issues or leaving you feeling highly stressed or unfulfilled, then it would be beneficial to your whole well-being to have a good hard look at the situation you're in and what you can do about it.

Firstly, set in motion a plan of action to prepare yourself for your next step. You are worthy of a job that suits you and your lifestyle. Decide what it is you want to pursue and go for it!! We all spend so much of our lives working, we ought to make it something we feel a sense of satisfaction and fulfilment from.

If you're feeling stuck in this area there are a lot of good books and resources out there to help guide you. If it's important to you, give it the attention it needs.

> *"If you take your eye off the ball, you're going to miss it, it'll go right past you. So stay focused!"*
> —Coral Emerson

Achievements:

What is it that you would like to achieve? Whether big

or small, start writing down all your hopes, dreams and goals.

Look at the timeline for achieving each goal. If you have a long to-do-list, and boy I know I do, break it down into smaller portions, for now just focusing only on the ones you want to prioritise. Get them all written down first, then create a separate list for those super important goals.

Next, pick one. Just choose one *really special* goal. Consider how you can progress forward to achieving this one goal, step by step. Write down the steps. If it helps, you can work backwards (from the goal to present time) so you can work out what needs to happen to get you there. Once you know what the steps are, make your goal more practical and easily achievable by doing just that first step. Even the greatest goal is achieved through simple daily habits. Accomplish it, and celebrate your first step forward. Continue this, step after step, and you will reach your objective.

If you get stuck on this at any time, I recommend you start reading about goal setting or talking to others who are natural goal setters and achievers. Learn from the best so that you can be your best too. Remember to prioritise where you put your creative energy so that general day-to-day duties don't diminish your goal.

Be proud of your achievements – no matter how small. An achievement is still an achievement.

Sometimes potential achievements look like challenges! When a challenge presents itself, you can either fight it or flow with it. The most attainable and balanced position is to Flow with it, with a Fighting Spirit!

Make your goals accountable.

For example, "I need to eat more fruit" would be achievable by saying, "I will eat three pieces of fruit a day." Now you have set a standard and a goal with a definite outcome.

"I want to lose weight" to "I'm going to lose 10kgs within 4 months."

"I need a holiday" to "I'm going to Hawaii next September."

Make a decision, make it clear, create a time frame, then work out how to achieve it. Start dreaming those dreams again and know they'll come true. It's all up to you.

Follow your heart and let your head work out the rest.

"Imagination – is the doorway to your success."
—Coral Emerson

Vision Board:

A Vision Board can be a very helpful tool in focusing on what's important to you.

Turn your attention to what you want in your life: happiness, love, a great career, a new car, good health, fitness, a family, to travel... whatever you would like to work towards in your future.

Start to collect images and words to create a Vision Board. This can be done with magazines and photographs, or images off the Internet. You can even design an online version. Now cut and stick, or copy and paste, and get your mind focused on a visual representation of what you are aiming for.

Place your Vision Board in a prominent place where you will see it daily. This task will help you to prioritise your goals, to get a clear mindset for what's important to you, and help to keep a strong focus on achieving your goals. Subconsciously you have decided what you would like in your life, and this is a visual representation of these deeper desires, bringing it to a conscious realisation. Therefore, it becomes a very subtle but powerful tool to assisting you on your path.

The Vision Boards I have created for myself over the years have all been so inspiring! I will sometimes do a new board each year, but often they last for longer than that, depending on what goals I've put onto it.

A Vision Board creates a daily visual reminder of everything that's truly important to me, where I want my focus to be, plus a deep sense of satisfaction at achieving my goals and following my dreams.

> "Take the bull by the horns and step forward and step up into your life."
> —Coral Emerson

Challenge and Reward:

The challenges that you set for yourself give you something to work towards, to overcome, to test your boundaries and your strengths. When you are making progress and achievements you must reward yourself!

Sounds exciting, huh?!

What's the best way to do this? Only you will know.

What is it that you desire and enjoy? What are life's simple pleasures to you? These are your rewards. Keep them healthy and wholesome, something that continues to enhance the life you are creating now.

Make a list of how you would like to reward yourself:

- ....
- ....
- ....

"I relish the challenge!"
—Coral Emerson

Fun and Excitement:

Put a bit of "spice" into your life and say: "I relish the challenge!" By doing this you will achieve a few things in one go. Not only will you have fun – something you deserve – but this will also help to build up your confidence. Plus, you'll fill the life-bank with awesome memories to look back on.

During this time of **Rebuild**, I began to do things I'd always wanted to do (or not, haha, but decided to anyway!). I did a variety of new things like skydiving, abseiling, getting on a stand-up paddle board. I went whale watching and pushed past my hesitations (due to the fact I'm prone to motion-sickness). I wanted to do it – so I did! I love whales and wildlife, so this was something really important to me. I took all precautions, worked my way through it, and had a wonderful time. Big tick off the Bucket List. Keen to do it again!

In writing this book, I am fulfilling a lifelong dream to become an author. Now let's get vulnerable here... my main aim in writing this book is to help others, but I may have to face rejection, criticism, and many other unpleasant responses. Hey I'm not perfect, I may not live up to others' expectations. I'm fully aware of this, but I'm going to do it anyway. Of course, the joy is, no one is perfect and no-one can fulfil all others' expectations. You can only but live to your own potential, be true to yourself, live your life, follow your dreams, and respect (and encourage) others to do the same. Be what it may.

During this important stage I made a decision to jump out of a plane! I planned to do my first skydive.

Woohoo! Not something I'd ever considered doing in my whole life until then. Being friends with skydivers over the last few years certainly had an influence on me... and I'm so glad I opened up my world to include something completely new, and definitely out of my comfort zone.

Basically, once I make a decision that I want to do something, I then find a way to do it. If I know it's going to scare the pants off me, I will look for a solution to combat those reactions in a positive way. I find that using relaxation techniques or altering how my brain reacts to certain situations is the key.

In regard to skydiving, rather than focusing on the fall, I focused on the fact that I was going to experience something out of this world, the closest thing to flying! Also, that I got to share this experience with one of my good friends, who was the tandem master. I focused on how amazing I was going to feel afterwards for having achieved something that had previously scared the crap out of me! I thought of how proud I would be of myself and that I would come away with a new sense of exhilaration and a heightened experience – literally. On a deeper level, while I was sitting in that plane getting ready to go, I visualised that we had angel wings, and somehow this gave a deep sense of calm.

Now, what is it that you would like to do? You don't have to go this extreme, of course... or you could go more extreme... whatever takes your fancy! Remember that being "adventurous" is simply trying something new. It doesn't matter if it's big or small, it's what's *amazing* to you.

Okay, what is it that you've always wanted to do that makes you feel both excited and that you'll poop yourself at the same time?! Haha, now you're thinking of some cool stuff, hey? Well, how about you give it a go?!!

Here's a list of popular choices:
- Skydiving
- Abseiling
- Remote expedition
- Acting on stage
- White water rafting
- Wake boarding
- Bungee jumping
- Whale watching
- Wildlife safari
- Singing
- Helicopter flight
- Climbing a mountain
- Public speaking
- Scuba diving
- Ride on a Harley

You might like to add some of your own:

- ....
- ....
- ....

> *"Do what makes you feel so damn good you glow."*
> —Coral Emerson

Sex:

A very intimate subject, but one that is important to delve into.

When we share ourselves with someone else on a sexual level, we also share on a more deeply intimate level, whether we're conscious of it or not. A part of who they are and who you are meets on a subconscious level. When this connection is in balance, it's a magical experience, but when it's out of balance, one person can be left feeling empty.

Look, I'm going to chat to you like I would a close friend – straight up and to the point! You may choose to do whatever you like in regard to sex, of course. Whatever you want to do with your body, and with who, is something only you can decide. But – this is your best friend stepping in here – if you are wanting to make significant changes in your life from now on, it's important to stay within your own morals and values, go with what "feels right" for you, and be safe at all times. When we are feeling lonely, lost or down, it can make us more vulnerable and it's only natural to want to reach out for some nurturing or satisfaction. Just check in with yourself the next time it comes up, to see if you are tyring to fill a void, or whether this is a healthy decision for you. Whatever choice you make is the right one for you, as long as you feel good.

If you are in a relationship and the intimacy between you needs a bit more passion and spark, then it's time to bring this important issue to the forefront and rebuild that connection with your partner. Making that extra effort definitely enhances the depth in a relationship and your bond with each other. "Making love" is the physical process of sharing love and showing love to each other. It is all about being open, giving and receiving, taking time to share yourself with each other in a way that is unique and special to you both. Not only do you deserve it, but so does your partner. And you can have a lot of fun in the process. Plus, the added benefits of feeling super relaxed, easing stress and tension, increasing the serotonin levels, and getting in a bit of extra exercise too!

If single, well you have a lot more freedom, but it still comes back to the basics: respect yourself and respect others. Your decisions on sex and intimacy clearly reflect your state of mind and speak volumes about the respect that you expect in the bedroom *and* in life.

Once a deed is done you can't take it back. So make it a good one! Keep all your choices in life, not just ones about sex, choices that you can be proud of and that improve your life. In this way your confidence and self-esteem will grow.

Above all, sex is meant to be pleasurable and enjoyable. If this is not the case, then something certainly needs to change. Naturally, it is a change that will reap many rewards. Making love to the right person is very healing and nurturing, and creates a deep connection and intense sense of well-being.

"There is magic in you. Let it sparkle."
—Coral Emerson

I Honour Myself:

This is the centre of everything!! Say these three words to yourself *every day*, in fact *several* times a day to start with: "I Honour Myself."

Let me explain why this is so amazing...

Believe it or not, "I Honour Myself" can be even more powerful than the more commonly used phrase of "I

Love Myself." Well, for starters, it's probably going to be a lot easier to say without feeling awkward. I know it is for me! The great part about it is this: to honour yourself is to love yourself completely, so you've got it all covered.

On a basic level, it is living by your moral standards, loving yourself for who you are, treating yourself with respect, honouring your heart, mind, body, and soul.

Now this is where it goes up a level, and this simple awareness can be life-changing. To truly honour yourself is to not let negative emotions overwhelm you and rule your life.

Consider this, if you are feeling frustrated, upset, angry, tense, then what are you doing to yourself? You are causing tension within your body, your body then reacts, it will increase inflammation, which increases pain, aches, and therefore even more tension in the body, all while a whirlwind of negative emotion courses through your entire being. To "honour yourself" is to let these unpleasant sensations leave you as soon as they come in (or as quickly as possible).

Hey, we all have this happen to us, me too, but the key is to let it go, or resolve it, as quickly as you can.

The first step is awareness… being aware that you are even feeling these things and being aware of the reactions in your body. As soon as you've **Realised** that negativity has entered your personal space be prepared to **Release** it, to let it go. You don't need it. It doesn't serve you well or contribute to your positive growth. Although these feelings came into you, it is you who is *holding onto* the negative thoughts and feelings.

Remember that if you are going to feel these things, it is also you who needs to dissipate them, to let them go. To do this is to Honour Yourself! For you have done the greatest thing you can do, to have a healthy and happy heart, mind, body, and soul.

I will say, this is the most important advice I have ever received! These three words "I Honour Myself" I hold close to my heart, and will do for the rest of my life!

Memorise and keep it in your soul forever.

"I Honour Myself"

Overview:

You have made tremendous progress in your own self transformation! Look at all you have achieved. The "new you" has arrived and is staying for good. You know you have the ability to change and mould your life the way you want it to be. These are the skills you need to carry you forward for the rest of your life! Rebuilding is a process that you can continue – you set the pace, you set the standard, you set the goals. And you have the ability to achieve them!

In Key 4 everything comes together. It is a time to **Refine** all that you know about yourself, all that you wish to continue striving for. It is your time to thrive! To live your life with a happy heart and have the tools in place to find your strength, when strength is called upon. This is the key to maintaining the life you've been looking for.

KEY POINTS

- Continue with any Key Points and Actions from Keys 1 and 2 that are still relevant
- Finding and keeping a good life balance is vital
- Your health and well-being are a priority

- Happiness – choose it and you will have it
- Social life – keep a connection to what's going on around you
- Opposites attract – try a whole new approach
- Career – important to do work that fits with your ethos and life
- Fun and excitement – bring some spice back into your life
- Essential Oil support: bergamot, cinnamon, lime, orange

KEY ACTIONS

- [ ] Find yourself – ask yourself the big questions, are you heading in the direction you want to go?
- [ ] Work towards important goals – plan a timeline
- [ ] Mini-makeover – have fun!
- [ ] Time out for you – plan a special treat
- [ ] Write down your achievements – be proud for all that you achieve, big or small
- [ ] Make a Vision Board – allow your true desires to flow out
- [ ] Challenge and Reward – set a challenge and create a reward
- [ ] "I HONOUR MYSELF" say it every day! Several times if need be

> "Look around you. Look beyond. Now look beyond where you've never looked before."
> —Coral Emerson

KEY 4

Refine

This is the final key to open the door to constant progress and future success.

Refining yourself, your life, is all about going that step further. Taking what you've managed to achieve so far and making it sparkle and shine.

To grow

To keep achieving

To continue moving towards your goals. Always!

This stage will become part of your life forever. It stops you from slipping backwards, or from living a life less than you should be.

You already have the resources, you know you can do it, because you've got this far. But we've got to keep the maintenance up! Just like with everything. Think about it... if we didn't look after our house or our car, it would fall apart or break down, right? Aha! Well, we're not going to let that happen to us.

We are now in the perfect position to halt issues as they arise. If we start to feel that something is not right, rather than running away, what we're going to do is pounce on it, pull it apart, poke it, prod it, decipher it, and go, "Hey, what's this? I'm putting a stop to it right now! What can I do about it?" And look for solutions immediately.

Guess what?! You've now taken the power out of the "issue" and given the power to yourself, because *you've* taken control. You *will* find a way to resolve it, no matter what it is. This is the KEY!

In **Refine** you keep learning new things about yourself. Your knowledge will grow and you will find that your confidence grows naturally along the way.

Consider the past, present and future...

On a basic level it can be viewed like this:

>PAST - Habits
>PRESENT - Issues
>FUTURE - Concerns

But it can be improved by looking at it like this:

>PAST - *Habits* can be changed
>PRESENT - *Issues* can be addressed as they arise
>FUTURE - *Concerns* let you know what you need to work on

If you deal with things as they surface you are actually very cleverly dealing with the past, present, and future all at once. Fantastic! Guaranteed results, and the benefit of getting one step closer to the *you* that you want to be, every time.

Is life perfect for me now? No, haha, and even if perfection were attainable, I wouldn't want it, because in *perfection* there are no *challenges*. And without challenges there is no growth.

> *"You're always, always, always going to be on your way to something more - always. And when you relax and accept that and stop beating up on yourself for not being someplace that you're not, and instead, start embracing where you are while you keep your eye on where you're going - now life becomes really, really, really fun."*
> —Abraham Hicks

Grow:

All life needs to grow: plants, animals, humans, our Earth, the solar system, the universe around us. In growth, we evolve. If we take part in directing our own growth, then we grow in the direction we desire.

Growth can often feel uncomfortable at the time, even painful. It depends on the lesson we need to learn as to the extent of it. But growth always results in reward and a sense of achievement. It is usually when we're looking back that we see it. Feel reassured that your period of intense growth will bring about positive change. Embrace the opportunity to grow.

> *"Unwind the colours of your soul by taking a journey you don't know."*
> —Coral Emerson

Weaknesses:

We all have them. But what do we do about them?

Even when you are at the stage of **Refine** - a lifelong state of refining your situation - your weaknesses will still show up from time to time to say hello. When this happens you may feel sad, frustrated, angry, rejected, upset, and all sorts of other emotions may surface. Some of your old ways, reactions, and habits may even kick in! Yeah, I go through this too. It's not much fun, but hey, it's just a natural part of life.

This is where we want to minimise the impact of that.

Okay, so something negative has just happened… and it's got to you.

Firstly, acknowledge it. See it for what it is. Basically, if something is making you feel a certain way you don't want to feel, you've got to **Realise** what it is. Where is this feeling coming from, and what is it related to?

Next, allow yourself to feel the emotion without beating yourself up about it. In this moment hold back the urge to express it… you just need to acknowledge it for now. Ideally you will be by yourself when you do this. If that's simply not possible, then just allow a few minutes to go internally while you sort this out. If you're with other people, explain you just need a moment, and walk outside or into another room. Give yourself some space. If you're at work, find a task that takes you away from others for a short while. You could even go to the restroom if it's your only escape.

If you're in a tricky situation where you cannot find space on your own, maybe you're on a bus, train or in a car, or stuck in a meeting, then this is a "quickie" version:

Ask yourself, "What is it that's *really* bugging me at the moment, why am I so upset by this? Can I do anything about it right now?" If not, then store it away to sort out later and immediately find the simplest way to relax and honour yourself. Take a few deep breaths and tell yourself, "I'm going to deal with this later." It's important to respect your right to have a mind and body that is not under constant stress. Reassure yourself that you will sort it out later, giving you freedom to continue on with your day as planned.

Finally, as soon as you can find the opportunity, give yourself some time to work through it as soon as possible, therefore diminishing, or even eliminating, its negative effect on you. You are honouring yourself by resolving this as efficiently as you can. Work through the current issue with the **Realise, Release, Rebuild, Refine** concept and it will help clear this for you very effectively.

If you do realise what has upset you, and you do have time to sort it out, go through the 4-step process of **Realise, Release, Rebuild, Refine** for that particular issue.

Remember: Get rid of it and/or grow from it. Either option will give you your strength back.

In basic steps

Having an overwhelming negative feeling?

1. Don't take any drastic action.
2. Understand this is a reaction. Don't beat yourself up about it; just know that you're going to work through it.
3. Start to process within yourself as to why you're having that kind of reaction.
4. Begin to resolve it as soon as you can.
5. If this is not possible at this time, look outwards – work on calming yourself down, listen to the sounds around you, bring your attention to the here and now. Slow your breathing.
6. Remember your divine right to be happy and to refuse to have stress in your body. This is your choice and a great gift to yourself. To Honour Yourself.

> *"Stress does not become me."*
> —Coral Emerson

The dreaded "S" word:

Another thing that can catch you off-guard is stress. It sneaks up quietly, and can do a fair bit of damage if you don't realise it early on. In fact, this has happened to me several times... I would find myself saying things like, "I'm so exhausted lately; work is really hectic, I can barely keep up; I just don't have any extra time; I'm feeling a bit flat, not sure why; the pain in my back is really bad at the moment; I haven't had a chance to do the things I enjoy, just don't know how I can do everything," etc.

The reasons... well it's rather multi-layered (as it often is), which means when this happens, I have to address a few different issues, and sometimes turn to the right people for the right support. And most importantly, use my own inner strength to push past barriers and realign my focus.

Stress management is essential. It is truly beneficial to get ourselves into a state of relaxation regularly. Otherwise, we will be in a constant 'flight and fight' mode. As you are probably aware, this causes all sorts of problems.

Life is meant to be enjoyed. When that stops happening, you've also got to stop yourself and ask why.

Sometimes you can be enjoying life just fine, but still experience stress. This is pretty common, and I can really relate to this. You know what, if life can be *better*, then make it better.

You are the most important person in your life. If you don't believe this, please go back to the start, and re-

read until you believe it! Tough love here, but trust me, it's a biggie in regard to your personal growth and the intrinsic joy you will reap out of life!

When I start worrying, or can feel stress building up, I now take it as a clue to fix something. For me, one of the main signs of stress is an increased level of pain in my upper back. During times of stress, I tend to get a flare-up from the pain caused by the car accident. Unfortunately stress increases inflammation in the body, and that in turn causes tension in the muscles and the pain becomes very difficult to manage. On a mental and emotional level, I can also get really uptight if I'm stressed, when normally I'm pretty chilled-out and relaxed. For a lot of people, the common symptoms are headaches, tight shoulders, shallow breathing, poor sleep, exhaustion… and sometimes there are no obvious physical symptoms, but rather emotionally-based symptoms like feeling frustrated, short-tempered, worried, anxious or unhappy.

Look for the signs, they're different for everyone, so work out what yours are. Also learn to know what your triggers are and you will start to notice the stress signal sooner and therefore be able to deal with it quicker.

I realised a very important connection in my own life… how stressed I was about the pain was almost as detrimental as the pain itself. High stress levels and pain are very much entwined, so if this is an issue for you too, I sincerely recommend you look into it more deeply and do everything you can to manage your stress reactions. It will help tremendously in the management of the pain. For some of us the pain may never go away, so this is particularly important in those circumstances. Good stress management truly does lead to reducing the effects of pain and increasing the pleasure of life again.

Research some relaxation techniques that you're comfortable with or give meditation a go. These can be very effective at dropping the stress levels and bringing a feeling of peace and calm. When you're in that calmer, more balanced space, you can deal with things so much more effectively.

Remember that diet and exercise also play a pivotal part in this process. It's easy to forget how vital that is when you're under pressure. The right foods can be so supportive, and the wrong foods can be damaging to our bodies and brains. Getting the body moving will trigger the production of endorphins, chemical messengers which help with improved feelings of well-being in general. Hey, I'll admit I'm not brilliant at exercise, but even a simple walk can work wonders. Or throw on some music and do a silly dance around the house. It doesn't really matter what it is, just make sure that body of yours has a chance to move and release tension.

Take a brief moment to look at the little things... a dewdrop glistening on a blade of grass, a ray of sunshine shining through the trees or buildings, how the books are stacked in the bookshelf, the intricate grain in a piece of wood, the colours in rocks and stones, unusual shaped leaves... notice the small things, look at them more closely. Allowing yourself a few moments of peace and quiet, even if it's only once a day, can really help to balance and re-energise.

Focus on a good sleep pattern and getting back to basics, essentially aiming for a balanced lifestyle (well, as much as is possible at the time). These are simple, but tried and true techniques to help reduce the effects of stress.

Quite frankly, I've realised the greatest fight is against myself; my emotions and how to handle them. When you start to acknowledge in fact that *it's all up to you*, how you're going to react, how you're going to deal with that situation, then you have discovered the ability to work with yourself on the path to consistent positive change. This is the greatest tool to get you through the rest of your life.

> *"It feels good to feel good!"*
> —Coral Emerson

It *feels* good to feel good! It really does, doesn't it?! Keep acknowledging that feeling and finding ways to recreate it.

> *"The difference between a fantasy and a reality is that the dream has an action plan"*
> —Kristy Barker – Mindset Coach

Follow your dreams:

Realise your dreams and have the courage to pursue them. Go for your goals.

Invest in yourself and your future. Learn, study, achieve, travel, love wholeheartedly... do whatever it is that you were meant to do and don't let anything hold you back. It is commonly said that the main regrets we have, are the things we didn't do. So, go and do the things you've always wanted to do.

If this has been troubling you, there could be many reasons why you're not fulfilling your dreams. If you feel like something has been holding you back, work out what those reasons are and don't let them stand in your way. Then you can celebrate as you start to tick those items off your Bucket List, one by one.

We've all got dreams and goals resting deep in our

soul. What are yours?

Big goals start with little steps. For every step, for every achievement, you are one step *further* than when you started. All achievements, no matter how small, are still achievements! And all dreams are worthy if they feel important to you. Honestly, in the big scheme of things, we're not on this earth for long, so we'd best make the most of it!

Please remember, while you're busy following your dreams, to always make time for your loved ones. Even the grandest goal should not detract from having quality time with those you love and letting them know how important they are to you. The special relationships around you are very precious... so be sure to treat them as such.

> *"Bad shit is gonna happen.*
> *Use it to fertilise your life."*
> —Coral Emerson

Issues:

When any issues arise – nip it in the bud.

Take action, source the most appropriate support and advice. Remember that although *you* know *you* better than anyone else, you do not always have all the answers. You may come across little hiccups along the way... hey, that's normal... that's life!

Apply your techniques:

Realise the issue and resolve to fix it

Release and let go of anything you don't need

Rebuild to create a positive result

Refine to continue living your life to the full

Take ACTION throughout each step!

That's the whole key to it. As you can see, each step requires an insight *and* an action. You've got to see it first, then do something about it. It's a very simple process for a very astounding result. Your well-being is your number one priority! And that's the way it should always be.

> *"Be true to you and all your dreams will come true."*
> —Coral Emerson

Live your truth:

Stay true to yourself and your own path.

There is no one like you – you are completely unique. What a treasure you are! Learn to love your differences, as they are what give you character and make you interesting. Your individuality is a gift. It is because of these qualities within us all that some of the greatest of inventions have been discovered. Because of our differences, we create art and architecture, music, scientific breakthroughs, new technology, medical marvels, movies, and so much more.

Do not deny the world all that you can offer. Do not deny yourself who you really are. You are important to others, and, strange as this may sound at first, you are important to you. It is *you* who decides how to treat your **HEART**, **MIND**, **BODY**, and **SOUL**. So yeah, don't take yourself for granted... you are awesome!

From here, you have the strength to give.

To give the best of you.

And this benefits not only yourself but everyone around you.

> *"Stop and smell the roses*
> *Look at the stars*
> *Find a place of peace*
> *Within yourself*
> *And within life*
> *You are at the heart*
> *Of Your life."*
> —Coral Emerson

A deeper connection:

Look at love in all its aspects... deeper, holistic, earthly...

Allow your soul to reach out and explore the connection between us all, the connection to life and the Earth we live on. Know that there is goodness in this world and be open to the very powerful positive energy that is available to us all. Search for the good and you will find it.

There are lots of things you can do to enhance this aspect of yourself, and there are many books, groups, and resources out there if you wish to know more. If you are drawn to it, then it is meant for you.

In its simplest form, to be thankful for what we have, to see beauty in ourselves, others and the world around us, to give and receive with love and kindness... this will connect you.

Living your life in a way that honours you is the greatest connection you can make. Your spiritual journey is a very personal one. Simply stay true to what it means to you.

And something that may surprise you is this:

Consider the 4 Elements of HEART, MIND, BODY, and SOUL. The essentials for balance! Here's the thing...

when you get Heart, Mind, and Body on track, your Soul is good, it all falls into place. The most spiritual thing you can do is to *live a life with love,* be true to yourself, be happy, have strength and courage. To Honour Yourself.

In this you Honour your Soul. And you will find a deep and real connection with yourself and everything around you.

> *"Do not go where the path may lead, go instead where there is no path and leave a trail."*
> —Ralph Waldo Emerson

Don't stop there:

Keep doing things you've never done before and relish in the challenge. Continue doing this. Don't stop because you're in a great place in your life, or a stable comfortable place, or for any other reason you may come up with. Life is for living, after all.

So, tick off that Bucket List and create new adventures to strive for!

> *"Anything that gets your blood racing is probably worth doing."*
> —Hunter S. Thompson

Sharing a personal experience...

How do I express this! Part way through writing this book I did something I never thought I'd do...

Skydiving!!!

I wrote this on the same day:

WOW! It's one way to blow your mind! And expand your experiences! I've just come back from the most exhilarating ride of my life. Diving 14,000ft over the Indian Ocean, taking in the beautiful countryside. The best view, one that kept changing - and growing! - before my very eyes.

Strapped to the Tandem Master, who is one of my best friends... feeling so secure, putting my trust completely in him and the situation... and sharing this amazing first-time experience with not only my gorgeous friend, but with the awesome skydiving team and the other brave souls on the plane with me, jumping for their first time too. Everyone appeared relaxed (albeit with an air of anticipation). Afterwards I had a bit of insight... I discovered one of the other guys jumping that day was really nervous. But he didn't let on! He put his fear aside and did it anyway! He dressed himself in a funny "Onesie" outfit and went for it! He had a very proud and excited wife waiting for him on the beach. I think that's awesome! Well done to him. My mum, who was watching me do my daring descent, loved that she got to share in this amazing moment with me.

When it came to the actual jumping out of the plane, I had to let go. Literally of course, haha, but most importantly, let go of any fears, or any perceived expectations, of everything!! I let go, trusted in the process and just let it happen. And it felt like everything went whoosh out of my mind, hahaha. I have never before had such a sensation! I can barely find the words. After a thrilling free-fall, the parachute opens and suddenly everything slows down... and I could take in all that was surrounding me... drinking in the beauty of the landscape, I felt so at peace, so relaxed and happy. I've looked back on the video, some parts are hilarious, but that moment is pure bliss.

As I leave the airport hangar, I think "What next?! How do I top that!!" So I come home to write... and share this with you.

> "Do not be pushed by your problems.
> Be led by your dreams."
> —Ralph Waldo Emerson

Overview:

So, when you get to the stage of **Refine**, is life perfect then?

Certainly not! Ahh, what's with all this effort then? Because life will be so much *better* from now on! And will continue to improve along the way, as you now have the tools to make that happen. You've discovered the 4 simple Keys to unlocking the life you want. Just keep those keys handy so you can use them any time you need.

Okay, so life isn't perfect. What is *perfect* anyway? And even when we do reach that level of existence which we may define as "perfect," it ultimately changes! For those who say, "There's no such thing as perfect," (and I've been one of them), I'm going to give another point of view… it does exist, there's a reason the word exists, but it's merely a *moment in time*, and your own *interpretation* of that moment in time. It passes. Precious perfect moments happen… and then they're gone. The most amazing part of it though, is that those moments become treasured memories.

The **Refine** stage is about being prepared for those changes that affect us and adapting as quickly and smoothly as possible. The basic 4-step system in this book will get you through, each and every time. Take each issue as it comes and fix it, ditch it, grow from it and get on with enjoying your life!

This is your time. And it's *your* life! It is important that you continue to stay on top of any issues that may arise, as well as enhancing your pleasure for life with fun and exciting things to do. It is always good to have the balance of work and play. Keep refining your life day by day and you will be the amazing person you've always wanted to be and live a life more deeply fulfilling than ever before.

KEY POINTS
- Continue with any Key Points and Actions from Keys 1, 2 and 3 that are still relevant
- Pull everything together to *refine* all that you know, and you will always stay on track
- Grow – and continue to grow to constantly improve your life
- Weaknesses – understand them and become stronger because of them
- Negativity – have techniques ready to beat this quickly
- Stress – combat this with the best tools that work for you. Don't let it control your life.
- Research meditation or relaxation techniques that resonate with you
- Follow your dreams – your dreams are worthy and you deserve to enjoy them
- Issues – look for solutions immediately to quickly resolve issues
- Stay true to yourself and your path – the key to fulfilment in life
- A deeper connection – stay connected to that which is meaningful to you

- Relish the challenge – thrive from the achievement
- Stay on track by using the resources available to you and keep refining your life each day
- Essential Oil support: chamomile, ginger, sandalwood, tangerine

KEY ACTIONS

☐ The *only* action required is to *take action* when required

> *"When one door closes, another opens; but we often look so long and so regretfully upon the closed door that we do not see the one which has opened for us."*
> —Alexander Graham Bell

CONCLUSION

The 4 Keys to *Open the Door to a New You* are now yours to use forever.

You may have read this book from start to finish, without pausing... and that is wonderful, I thank you from the bottom of my heart for sharing this journey with me and I hope you have found something within these pages that resonates with you.

To get the results you want, allow yourself time to go through the processes at your own pace, along your own path, in your own way.

Time is a healer, and when combined with action, it can be truly rewarding. As we know, time will pass anyway, but if we utilise it to create change, then change will inevitably happen.

If you are the one directing it, you will go in the direction you want. To live the life, you've always wanted!

This is the secret to remember:

4 KEYS
- **REALISE**
- **RELEASE**
- **REBUILD**
- **REFINE**

Realise and recognise what's going on and take action to resolve it

Release and let go of anything negative surrounding you, and within you, as necessary

Rebuild to work towards your goals, and build the life you want

Refine all the time, so that your life and surroundings reflect the you that *you* want to be

4 ELEMENTS
- **HEART**
- **MIND**
- **BODY**
- **SOUL**

It's all about dealing with challenges effectively. So, when issues come up, you have the 4 Keys in place to know how to deal with them, and the 4 Elements to keep everything balanced.

This simple but powerful method will enhance your life quality, not only for now, but forever.

You will never have to feel like you are stuck ever again. If you're not where you want to be in life, be the change that you wish to see. There are many options in life. **If you can't see your options, create them.**

Be the fabulous, gorgeous, sexy you, that you've always wanted to be!

"A book is a key that opens the door to Narnia."
—Chandler Bolt

DID YOU ENJOY THIS BOOK?

Thank you for reading this book. It means so much to me, and I sincerely hope you've found something useful.

If you enjoyed reading this book, please leave a review on Amazon.

Thanks again for your support.

Lots of love

Coral x

Contact Information

Email: coralemersonauthor@gmail.com
Facebook: @coralemersonauthor

ABOUT THE AUTHOR

Coral Emerson lives in the beautiful Southwest region of Western Australia, a country girl at heart with a deep love of life! She is a proud mum to one daughter, and together they make a rather cheeky pair, often mistaken for sisters… plus a shared sense of humour that's suspiciously hereditary.

She is passionate about contributing to positive change in this world, true love, compassion, and creating happiness. Coral finds pleasure in the simple things in life… stopping to smell the roses, being in nature, photography, chilling out with a good Netflix series and spending quality time with family and friends.

Coral is an advocate for FND (Functional Neurological Disorder). Having been diagnosed with the condition since 2018, but living with it for several years prior, she wants to help others, including the wider medical community, in understanding FND and being aware of the symptoms to aid in diagnosis and management. To find out more about FND head to: https://fndhope.org/

Coral has dreamed of being an author for as long as she can remember. Her desire to help others was the inspiration behind this book. She felt the best way to honour the knowledge gained from falling flat on her face, was to step up, reach out, and share everything she could to support others on their journey too.

LINKS

These are a few of my favourite things:

Pleasant Events Schedule
 www.healthnetsolutions.com/dsp/PleasantEventsSchedule.pdf

Corrynne's Natural Skincare
 www.soaps.net.au

Protein Powder
 www.bulknutrients.com.au

Turmeric Latte
 turmericdirect.com.au

The Style Counsellor
 @stylecounsellorciara (Facebook)
 @the_style_counsellor (Instagram)

Big thanks to:

Self-Publishing School

Cover design: Fiverr - germancreative

Editing: Elaine Roughton
 h.elaine.roughton@gmail.com

Layout & formatting: Kingfisher Design
 www.kingfisher-design.com

Photography: Milena di Latte Photography
 @milenadilattephotography (Facebook)
 @milena_di_latte_photography (Instagram)

SELF-PUBLISHING SCHOOL

NOW IT'S YOUR TURN

Discover the EXACT 3-step blueprint you need to become a bestselling author in 3 months.

Self-Publishing School helped me, and now I want them to help you with this FREE resource to begin outlining your book!

Even if you're busy, bad at writing, or don't know where to start, you CAN write a bestseller and build your best life.

With tools and experience across a variety of niches and professions, Self-Publishing School is the *only* resource you need to take your book to the finish line!

DON'T WAIT

Say "YES" to becoming a bestseller:

https://self-publishingschool.com/friend/

Follow the steps on the page to get a FREE resource to get started on your book and unlock a discount to get started with Self-Publishing School.

www.ingramcontent.com/pod-product-compliance
Lightning Source LLC
Chambersburg PA
CBHW050316010526
44107CB00055B/2268